CLASSIC CYCLE CLIMBS

The Bristol-Bath Region

50

CLASSIC CYCLE CLIMBS

The Bristol-Bath Region

J.J. Wheeler

THE CROWOOD PRESS

First published in 2016 by
The Crowood Press Ltd
Ramsbury, Marlborough
Wiltshire SN8 2HR

www.crowood.com

British Library Cataloguing-in-Publication Data
A catalogue record for this book is available from the British
Library.

ISBN 978 1 78500 131 4

Dedication
For my dad, whose wheel was the first I tried to follow. And to
Richard and Colin, whose wheels I couldn't.

Photographs
Climbs 13, 14, 16, 35, 36 and cover © John Meredith;
climb 26 © Lee Montgomery.

Typeset by Jean Cussons Typesetting, Diss, Norfolk
Printed and bound in India by Replika Press Pvt Ltd

CONTENTS

Overview map	6
About the author	8
Acknowledgements	8
About the book	9
Introduction	10
Technical matters	12
The climbs	16

1.	Alfred's Tower	18
2.	Ayford Lane	20
3.	Bowden Hill	22
4.	Brassknocker Hill	24
5.	Bridge Valley Road	26
6.	Bristol Hill	28
7.	Broadoak Hill	30
8.	Burrington Combe	32
9.	Castle Road	34
10.	Charlcombe Lane	36
	On climbing hills	38
11.	Cheddar Gorge	42
12.	Claverton Hill	44
13.	Crowcombe Hill Road	46
14.	Dead Woman's Ditch	48
15.	Dundry Lane	50
16.	Dunkery Beacon	52
17.	East Dundry Road	54
18.	Ebbor Gorge	56
19.	Gare Hill	58
20.	Gold Hill	60
21.	Harptree Hill	62
22.	High Street	64

23.	Hinton Hill	66
24.	Holt Road	68
25.	Langridge Lane	70
	How cyclists conquered Britain's hills	72
26.	Lansdown Lane (Weston Hill)	76
27.	Lansdown Road	78
28.	Margaret's Hill	80
29.	Mere Hill	82
30.	New Road	84
31.	Newtown	86
32.	Old Bristol Road	88
33.	Park Hill	90
34.	Park Street	92
35.	Porlock Hill	94
36.	Porlock Toll Road (New Road)	96
37.	Prospect Place	98
38.	Rosemary Lane	100
39.	Shaft Road	102
40.	Shipham Road	104
41.	Smitham Hill	106
42.	Steway Lane	108
43.	The Wrangle	110
44.	Two Trees	112
	From Taunton to Bath by bicycle	114
45.	Vale Street	116
46.	Westfield Lane	118
47.	Widcombe Hill	120
48.	Winford Lane	122
49.	Winsley Hill	124
50.	Woods Hill	126
	Local bike shops	128

Bath and Bristol Cycle Climbs

1 Alfred's Tower

2 Ayford Lane

3 Bowden Hill

4 Brassknocker Hill

5 Bridge Valley Road

6 Bristol Hill

7 Broadoak Hill

8 Burrington Combe

9 Castle Road

10 Charlcombe Lane

11 Cheddar Gorge

12 Claverton Hill

13 Crowcombe
    Hill Road

14 Dead Woman's
    Ditch

15 Dundry Lane

16 Dunkery Beacon

17 East Dundry Road

18 Ebbor Gorge

19 Gare Hill

20 Gold Hill

21 Harptree Hill

22 High Street

23 Hinton Hill

24 Holt Road

25 Langridge Lane

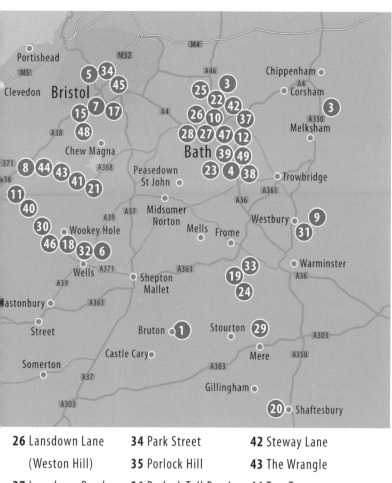

26 Lansdown Lane
    (Weston Hill)

27 Lansdown Road

28 Margaret's Hill

29 Mere Hill

30 New Road

31 Newtown

32 Old Bristol Road

33 Park Hill

34 Park Street

35 Porlock Hill

36 Porlock Toll Road
    (New Road)

37 Prospect Place

38 Rosemary Lane

39 Shaft Road

40 Shipham Road

41 Smitham Hill

42 Steway Lane

43 The Wrangle

44 Two Trees

45 Vale Street

46 Westfield Lane

47 Widcombe Hill

48 Winford Lane

49 Winsley Hill

50 Woods Hill

ABOUT THE AUTHOR

Joseph's love for bicycles and bicycling began in the mid-1980s when he saw his first mountain bike in a cycle shop in Cheltenham while studying for a Fine Art degree. He bought it and spent his weekends for the rest of his studies riding and exploring the nearby Cotswold hills.

In 1988 he travelled to London where he worked as a cycle courier, clocking up 60 miles a day on a second-hand Raleigh road bike. Two years later, Joseph moved with his partner, Jenny, to Bath where he worked as a bicycle mechanic for a few years. Then, along with a bit of amateur racing for local teams, he began a full-time career as an artist and illustrator.

Now with a young son and alongside his work as an established illustrator, he continues to ride, fettle and occasionally race his bikes around the countryside and hills of his adopted home in Somerset.

ACKNOWLEDGEMENTS

I've ridden a lot of miles in the search, discovery and detailing of the climbs that make up this book. It's true, many I fought alone, but I've also battled my way up a good number in the welcome company of brave friends who often had no idea of the horrors that awaited them.

So to those cycling accomplices, thanks! To Lee Montgomery, who must never have thought his first year of 'proper' cycling would include some of the very steepest hills in Somerset (some more than once) and who did some sterling work with the camera on a few of them. Also to Miles Peyton, whose endless patience when venturing twice into Dorset in search of the 'missing hill' that we never found, deserves a special mention. Thanks to Miles too for his '116 per cent'!

A very big and special thank you also to friend and photographer John Meredith who took time out with his camera and his bicycle to meet me at some of the more remote locations for this book, as well as taking some outstanding pictures – at least once in the most trying of conditions.

Thanks also to Bob Latchem and Victoria Ratcliffe of Somer Valley CC, whose impromptu and unexpected morning tour across the Mendips found me Two Trees when I had nearly given up hope. And thanks to the nurse at Frome Hospital who repaired my eye following a very painful and incapacitating encounter with a piece of grit.

A really big thank you to my partner Jenny who put up with it all for thirteen months and to my son Louis who watched enthusiastically as it took shape.

And finally, I'd like to say a huge thank you to Sholto Walker, without whom absolutely none of this would have been remotely possible.

ABOUT THE BOOK

The climbs in this book are ordered alphabetically. Each description starts with a table of acts about the climb, including the address of a local café or tearoom where tired riders can compare their own experience over a tea or coffee and slice of cake.

Difficulty	⊙⊙⊙⊙⊙⊙⊙⊙⊙⊙
Distance	2km
Av. Gradient	11%
Max. Gradient	20%
Height Gain	226m
Start Point	Beck Side. GR: 235 822 (OS Landranger 96)
Local Cafés	The Coach House Cafè Ford Park, Ulverston, LA12 7JP ☎ 01229 581666 www.ford-park.org/uk/cafe,asp

A map shows the start and finish point of the climb and the route it follows. We would recommend taking an OS map or a GPS system to help in plotting your route in more detail.

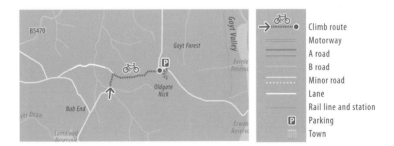

At the end of the book is a list of bike shops in the region. Each shops relates to one or more of the climbs listed in the book, so there will be one nearby if you are in need of spares, repairs or just good local advice.

INTRODUCTION

It was August 1976. I was ten. Up ahead, through tear-filled eyes I watched miserably as my best friend Richard and his dad pulled inexorably away, working their pannier-laden bikes up the side of one of the biggest hills the French countryside near Cherbourg in Northern France could chuck at us. Just ahead, with me on his wheel, my dad toiled stoically, trying to ignore my whimpers and whinings as he concentrated on the silent fight being waged in his sleep-starved head to get himself and his over-geared, second-hand Sun ten-speed to the top of the hill before he stopped on the spot, threw the whole lot in the ditch and announced he was taking the first ferry back to Southampton.

The four of us were on a cycling holiday and things had begun badly. The day before, in a spectacular and not untypical failure of planning, we had arrived in Cherbourg to discover that it was a bank holiday and every guesthouse and hotel in Northern France was jammed to the rafters with French holiday-makers. Consequently we had spent a chilly and rainy night swathed in our voluminous cycling capes trying to snatch a few hours sleep amongst the discarded beer cans, carrier bags and roadside detritus of a tatty strip of woodland beside a French B-road somewhere just outside Cherbourg. The experience had left none of us feeling ready (if we ever were) for the 30-mile ride we had planned for that day. It had done nothing either for the chest-aching homesickness to which I was then so often prone.

So as the new morning sun began to trickle through the leaves and branches, we had opened bleary eyes, extracted ourselves from our condensation-soaked capes and pulled our bikes from the undergrowth where we had resignedly let them fall in the unfamiliar woodland dark the night before. Apart from just going home, the only thing on our minds that chill, damp early August morning was to get out of that fetid wood, warm up and find something to eat.

But it was that hill nearly forty years ago that stuck hardest in my memory on that day. The tiredness, the misery of my freezing hands, the hunger, the pain in my legs, the sight of my best friend pulling away from me, the sense of defeat and hopelessness as I rode alone, my only thought the desperate wish to be anywhere but on that terrible hill, at the back. Last. It was a defining moment.

After that otherwise completely idyllic week-long adventure in Northern France I didn't really ride a bike again until my early twenties when I found myself, in a late-80s post-degree career hiatus, weaving around London as a cycle courier, any memories, sore or otherwise, of French hills by then so distant as to be forgotten.

Forgotten that is until I came to bumpy Somerset. It was here in 1989 that I pitched up with my bike and a keen ambition, inspired by Channel 4's new interest in professional cycle sport, to try a bit of amateur racing. It was here too that I re-discovered hills. And it was here I stumbled upon the still-smouldering ashes of my private defeat on that little hill in Northern France. Failure, I resolved, on these new English hills was no longer an option. But my re-discovery of cycling and its inevitable hills was to be a painful journey. I began at first alone, on over-sized gears, straining to turn cranks up steep muddy lanes, often finding myself grinding to a halt on the steepest parts of the toughest climbs and shamefacedly pushing my bike alone the rest of the way. I then graduated in a year or two to finding I could hold my own in a group of decent club-riders on the hardest of local hills.

So now, after many thousands of miles riding these roads and climbing their hills and after several summer seasons racing and occasionally competing in the local hill climbs, I find the glowing recollections of one of the best holidays a ten-year-old boy can have remain intact, while the misery of those five minutes on that Northern French hill in 1976 has been expunged finally and for ever. In fact, nearly forty years later, I find I've even managed to write a book celebrating fifty of the toughest.

Technical Matters

THE TERRAIN

As areas of England go, Bristol and the South West are not enormously hilly. There are areas where big hills certainly predominate, most notably Exmoor, the north-eastern corner of which features in this collection. While the Mendips also harbour some impressive challenges, Exmoor can probably hold its own amongst the toughest, in terms of their exposed nature, their length and their steepness, of any in England. Generally though, with a few notable exceptions, most of the hills in this book are manageable by anyone with good fitness, riding an adequately geared bicycle and with sufficient resolve. Getting up them quickly is of course quite another matter.

GRADIENTS

You'll notice this book is full of endless references to gradients. Satellite-linked cycle-computers and barometric altimeters have made this possible. In the recent past, unless the local council had installed a sign, cyclists had no precise idea of how steep any hill was. In fact, since the introduction of this technology it has become apparent that a lot of these warning signs are woefully inaccurate. They may give a driver adequate notice that they'll need to take extra care, but when a claimed 15 per cent hill has clearly taken no account of the 100-metre bit that touches 20 per cent near the top, you know that not only are the signs usually just estimates or averages at best, you can also be sure they haven't been thinking of cyclists when they put them up.

I quickly noticed when I was researching this book that almost without fail the most popular websites that allow cyclists to upload their ride data significantly underestimate gradients. This has something to do with the shortness of most British hills as well as the way these sites extract data, often missing or failing to record short sections of a climb or even, on some of the shortest climbs, barely reporting a gradient at all. All of the gradients I give are taken from my bike-mounted, barometric-equipped Garmin. While I know, due to its own idiosyncrasies these may not always be precise, they will still give people a very good understanding of what they are going to encounter on the road.

GEARING

As with other aspects of cycling, what is otherwise a perfectly understood subject when applied to bicycles has become imbued with myth and unfounded theories. Happily however, with the increased application of science to the engineering and physiological aspects of cycling, particularly at the elite competition level, a few valuable facts have emerged. Perhaps the most important of these is that on any hill over about 200m, lower gears are quicker. Assuming you can do it at all, no amount of heaving your way to the top of a 2km 9 per cent climb on a fifty-three tooth chainring will get you up quicker than if you select a far smaller gear, spend less time out of the saddle and learn to spin the pedals faster. This will save your legs, probably save your knees and most importantly, save you time.

This is not to say higher gears aren't quicker. At any given cadence (see below) they obviously are, but the tendency for cyclists to select big gears regardless of their ability to actually turn them at anything like an efficient cadence is legendary. This is probably a habit that particularly afflicted a slightly earlier generation of cyclists before lower geared compact transmissions and mountain bikes were widely available, but nevertheless the principle is still true. As you get fitter and stronger, you'll then find you are able to use a bigger gear, but without changing your cadence. This is how you'll get up the hill quicker.

Hills shorter than 200m are often an exception and can be ridden – by those who want to – as a sprint or 'power climb'. Here the rider works, out of the saddle, pushing a bigger gear, at or close to their maximum effort (anaerobically) all the way to the top. You'll find a few climbs in this collection that can be ridden this way. Be aware though, this type of climbing is inefficient and uses a lot of energy. On a long ride you should be very careful how often you do it.

TERMINOLOGY

There are a few words and phrases I use in this book that most seasoned cyclists will be familiar with. But for those less used to the language, here's a brief run-through.

Attack
Approach the hill (or part of it) aggressively. In cycle racing, also used to describe a sudden effort by one rider or group of riders to move away from the other rider or riders.

Break
Short for 'breakaway' in cycle racing. A group of riders that has moved ahead of the main bunch, often as the result of an attack.

Bunch

The peloton or main group of riders.

Cadence

Pedalling rate in rpm (revolutions per minute). Research has discovered that the most efficient cadence on a flat road is somewhere between 80 and 110 rpm. This apparently wide range allows for differing physiological factors in individuals as well as the vagaries of the terrain they may be riding over. When climbing you should expect your cadence to fall to between 60 and 80 rpm. If it falls much below this for any significant length of time and you're already on your bottom gear, then you should consider getting some lower gears.

Drag

Slightly steeper than a false flat (see below), but usually undemanding if it's not too long. Probably between 3 and 5 per cent. May be a problem if encountered immediately before a large climb.

False flat

A very shallow up-hill gradient, no more than 2 or 3 per cent. Not necessarily enough to immediately notice, but if it's long enough, very wearing. If it features in the approach to a hard climb and is long, like the drag (above), it can be a significant factor.

Steady

An even cadence, not necessarily slow, but remaining as comfortable as possible. Usually in the saddle.

THE CLIMBS

While all the climbs in this book offer a challenge, this is not the only reason they have been chosen. Certainly some are very demanding, but many are also worth riding for other reasons. Several offer glorious views of this beautiful part of England, while others are in an area linked closely to interesting local or social history. As you'd expect in such a lovely area, folded in places so deeply and so richly grained with the history of its inhabitants, a few of these climbs can offer all these things at once - a tough physical challenge, a glorious view and all while telling an excellent story.

I have graded each hill by difficulty with a mark out of ten. For two I have gone further and added a star to their maximum rating to set them apart and denote a further level of difficulty. I'm confident that these hills rank among the toughest in the region and cyclists should only attempt them clear in the knowledge of what they are likely to face.

Although I think a grading system is essential in an exercise like this, not to mention fun, it's perhaps not surprising that measuring a hill's toughness by numbers relative to others is more difficult than it sounds. Yes, I know there are various systems and formulas out there and apparently some work very well, but it has to be said, in the end, hills just don't conform readily to strict mathematical formulas. Most experienced cyclists know that some hills, regardless of their measured length or relatively moderate gradient are always just grindingly hard and conversely some hills that appear tough on paper can almost be a joy to ride. So with that in mind, I have exercised a fair degree of judgement, tinged inevitably with some subjectivity. I have also taken into account on every one, along with gradient and length, other crucial factors such as road surface and condition and how exposed a climb might be. In determining the difficulty of a climb, these features can be nearly as important as the bald figures.

You'll notice too that the lowest score in this collection is 4, an honour held by just one of the climbs. This is deliberate because I have made an effort to include, in addition to what I hope are all the hardest climbs in the region, only hills that offer at least a moderate challenge to any rider. I have deliberately excluded climbs that while they might be attractive or interesting, just don't rank high enough on the difficulty score. A hill really can't be considered a 'climb' unless it inspires at least a modicum of fear in the heart of the person about to start up it.

Many of the climbs in this collection are entirely new to me. I have hunted them out on maps, from reading what others have said, or just by exploring likely areas on a hunch. Other hills I know well. I've lost count of the times I've either ridden or raced up them. But despite the collective hours of torture they have meted out to my legs and lungs over the years, they hold mostly happy memories. Some I have revisited after many years of being away to find, like renewing an old but difficult friendship, the little idiosyncrasies I thought I'd forgotten, come back still to challenge and provoke.

Needless to say, I will have missed some hills. Among these a few, I'm sure, deserved inclusion. So if your favourite hill hasn't appeared, then my apologies; it either didn't make the grade or I never found it. My last words go to anyone who says any of these climbs are 'easy' – If it's easy, then you're not going fast enough!

I. ALFRED'S TOWER

Difficulty	◉◉◉◉◉◉◉◉○○
Distance	2.2km
Av. Gradient	8%
Max. Gradient	22%
Height Gain	157m
Road Surface	Moderate/Poor
Start Point	Bottom of Kingsettle Hill, approx. 1.5m south of South Brewham and approx. 5km east of Bruton GR: ST724345
Local Café	Cat's Café, 23 High Street, Bruton BA10 0AH ☎ 07850 684129

As a climb, Kingsettle Hill is known locally as 'Alfred's Tower'. This refers to King Alfred's Tower, the 49m Georgian monument that rises from its summit. For anyone cycling in the area, Alfred's Tower rarely leaves the consciousness for long. It dominates the landscape from almost every direction and provides a regular reminder of the challenge that awaits any cyclist prepared to brave the ascent of its western side. The gently rising approach to the tower could give you a false sense of security, but be prepared. The real challenge comes later on up the road when the climb hits you in stages with each harder than the previous and each robbing you of strength for the next.

THE CLIMB

Kingsettle Hill begins very slowly and you'd be forgiven for wondering what all the fuss is about as the road continues more or less level for the first several hundred metres. Then a false flat starts to make its presence felt. This continues with a short 5 per cent interlude before settling down again to around 3 per cent. After about a kilometre, the gradient starts to rise noticeably and as you pass a cottage on the left, this early dig hits a peak of around 9 per cent. Then there is a short respite where the gradient lessens before kicking again and rising to about 13 per cent as you pass a short terrace of cottages on your left.

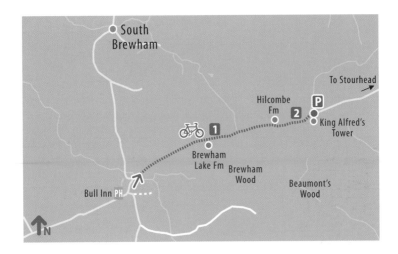

Now the fun really begins and you'll need to dig deep here because the road rises up very suddenly and if you've done the earlier part of the hill wrong, you may not have the legs for this last 600m. As the climb rounds the bend, it quickly ramps up to 17 per cent before dropping briefly to about 11 per cent. The hill then launches skyward to touch 22 per cent, backing off momentarily before finally, in a seemingly last-ditch effort to crush your spirit along

with your legs, it hits you with another 300m that again touches 22 per cent. The top, when finally gained, levels out mercifully quickly near the foot of the tower.

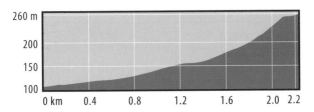

2. AYFORD LANE

Difficulty	⬤⬤⬤⬤⬤⬤⬤◯◯
Distance	1.3km
Av. Gradient	13%
Max. Gradient	25%
Height Gain	108m
Road Surface	Poor
Start Point	At bridge, Ayford Lane, St Catherine's Valley. Approx. 80m north of junction with St Catherine's Lane, approx. 3km north of Batheaston. GR: ST773709
Local Café	The Raft Café Boat, Tyning Road, Bathampton, Bath BA2 6TQ ☎ 07733 336989

The two big climbs of St Catherine's Valley have much in common. Ayford Lane and its slightly more refined sister Steway Lane (Climb 42), further down the valley, both share a confusing feel of rural isolation despite being just a few kilometres from the

City of Bath. Both also have a road surface that in wet weather will test your ability to stay upright while scaling a 25 per cent slope and both climbs lurch and scramble their way up shattered tarmac from the valley bottom, under a dark canopy of trees. But it has to be said, Ayford Lane is the darker and rougher of the pair. Further up the valley and more distant from Bathford, this climb is reached, appropriately enough, down a steep, crumbling piece of tarmac and over a small bridge that delivers you to the bottom of the hill.

THE CLIMB

From the start you'll probably notice the

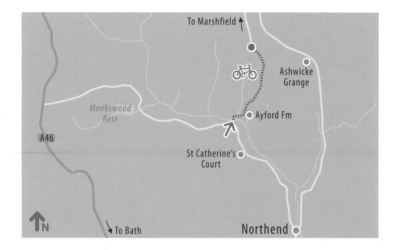

mud that collects at the bottom here. It's mostly heaped up in the middle of the road, so some judicious picking your way around it as you negotiate the early 20 per cent-plus gradient will be required. Fresh legs at this early stage will mean this is unlikely to be too much of a challenge and when the slope reduces momentarily you can take the opportunity to settle into a rhythm of sorts as, when the road turns up again, the pattern for the next kilometre or so begins to reveal itself. From here on there is no respite until you're nearly at the top. The gradient for the next 800m bounces between a shade under 20 per cent to around 25 per cent and even in dry weather you'll find much of the often broken surface is littered with mud and gravel that will have your back wheel spinning as you grind to a near stop on the steepest parts.

With about 300m to go, you'll feel the gradient finally easing as it drops to around 8 per cent. This will take you to the top of the climb and the finish beside a long tarmac drive to your left.

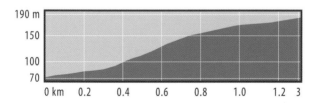

3. BOWDEN HILL

Difficulty	⊙⊙⊙⊙⊙⊙○○○○
Distance	2.1km
Av. Gradient	8%
Max. Gradient	16%
Height Gain	131m
Road Surface	Good
Start Point	The Wharf, approx. 600m east of Lacock, east end of bridge before Bewley village. GR: ST923680
Local Café	King John's Hunting Lodge Tea Room, 21 Church Street, Lacock, Wiltshire SN15 2LB ☎ 01249 730313

The fusty, dusty and eminently filmic National Trust village of Lacock is near where we begin this climb. Take the lane east from the village, past Lacock Abbey, where you'll see across the meadow the great leaded medieval oriel window that featured in the first photographic plate ever made. Shortly after the bridge, our ascent begins.

THE CLIMB

Although the first kilometre of Bowden Hill starts calmly enough, be warned, the hill is just toying with you on its lower slopes. There is a moderate gradient to start, which rises briefly but noticeably as the lane enters Bewley. Things then settle as you leave the village, only to dig in again as a short kick takes you momentarily past 7 per cent. The gradient yet again teasingly backs off up to a large drive entrance on the right where the road bends left. It is only here, after this initial light workout that the climbing gets more serious and the proper hard work begins.

As you round the bend, the gradient quickly steepens to around 16 per cent and doesn't drop below 10 per cent until you reach the church of St Anne, 600m further up the hill and still well out of sight. When you reach the church, count the worst of the hill as done. As you pass the common on the right and your legs savour this welcome drop in resistance, you might think that the road, for just a moment, has levelled out

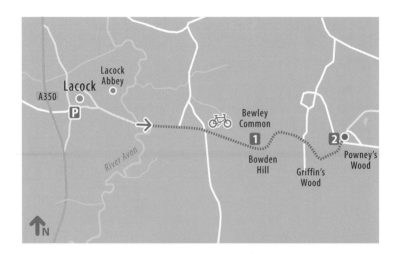

completely. But don't relax too much: 300m ahead, the climb rounds a final bend and, once again, you'll feel the gradient increase.

Although it's just 8 per cent at its worst here, the previous 2km will mean this last 250m will not go unnoticed. Consider the hill over a little way past the park entrances to your left and right.

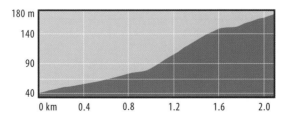

4. BRASSKNOCKER HILL

Difficulty	⬤⬤⬤⬤⬤⬤⬤◑○○
Distance	1.1km
Av. Gradient	10%
Max. Gradient	20%
Height Gain	116m
Road Surface	Good
Start Point	Bottom of Brassknocker Hill junction with A36 Warminster Road approx. 700m east of Monkton Combe. GR: ST781621
Local Café	The Angelfish, Brassknocker Hill, Monkton Combe, Bath BA2 7JD ☎ 01225 723483

In 1990 the Tour of Britain (then the Kellogg's Tour of Britain) came up this hill. They had set off from Brighton earlier that day and with the finish a few miles further on in Bath, Scottish Tour de France mountain legend Robert Millar broke from the lead group as they neared the steepest part of the climb. Only Federico Echave could stay with him that day, but it was Millar who took the points over the top.

The race was back three years later and this time it was Australian Phil Anderson who got to the top first. I know because I was standing on the bend watching him charge past. And I swear he was grinning.

These two events helped seal Brassknocker's reputation amongst local cyclists. But this handsome climb with the intriguing name, first striding and then twisting its way up the valley side, has always held a special place in the hearts (and legs!) of local riders.

THE CLIMB

At 15 per cent almost from the start, this climb is steep and your legs will get no decent respite until the gradient finally starts to slacken after the last bend at the top. 200m from the start, the gradient backs off a little as you pass a crossroads, but as the road starts to rise again and the landscape drops away from you to the left, the gradient steadily increases again. The climb peaks at 20 per cent on the first of the sharp

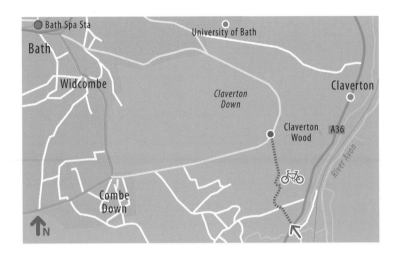

bends, but it is this long steep approach, visible to the rider for most of its length, that really sets the agenda.

For around 250m, through these two final bends, the gradient hovers at between 15 and 20 per cent. Still in the trees, the hill finally starts to back off as you approach the straight run to the finish. By the time you reach the end at the mini roundabout, you'll be spinning up a gentle and very welcome 3 per cent drag.

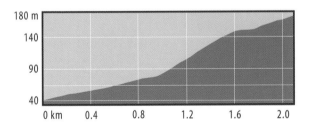

5. BRIDGE VALLEY ROAD

Difficulty	◯◯◯◯◯◯◯◯◯◯
Distance	0.8km
Av. Gradient	7%
Max. Gradient	9%
Height Gain	62m
Road Surface	Good
Start Point	Junction of A4 Portway and A4176 Bridge Valley Road, Clifton, Bristol. GR: ST563733
Local Café	Café Retreat, Durdham Down, Stoke Road, Bristol BS9 1FG ☎ 01179 238186

It's 10 September 2014 and Stage 4 of the Tour of Britain is charging into Bristol. After setting off from Worcester that morning, 183km of racing has brought them, via Bristol's spectacular Avon Gorge, to the bottom of Bridge Valley Road. In sight of Brunel's famous suspension bridge, this climb will prove decisive for the young Polish rider Michał Kwiatkowski. His brilliant attacking riding on this climb and through the last 400m over the top and through Clifton Downs will see him catch the break and win the stage in a spectacular dash for the line. By the end of the day he will be in

the Yellow Jersey for the start of the following day's stage from Exmouth.

Bridge Valley Road is no monster. Less than a kilometre long, it snakes its way up the side of the Avon Gorge, winding steadily up to Bristol Zoo and the Clifton Downs. If you don't fancy hurting yourself then stay in a low gear and this climb shouldn't raise an excessive sweat. On the other hand, you may want to have a go at Michał Kwiatkowski's Tour of Britain time to the top; he did it in 1 minute 33 seconds. If you beat that then you'll deserve a hearty pat on the back, but don't forget, for it to be truly impressive, you'll also need to have just raced 183km from Worcester.

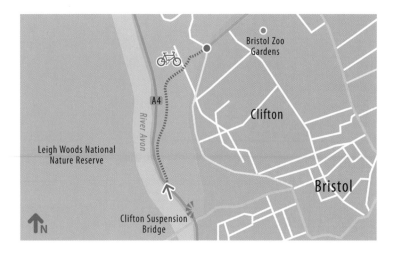

THE CLIMB

From the traffic lights at the bottom, the first 250m stretch of Bridge Valley Road sweeps you round a gentle right-hand bend at a not excessive gradient of 9 per cent. If you keep it steady from there, that's the hardest you'll have to work all the way to the finish line 600m further up the road. From this first bend, the climb cuts across the gorge's contour lines at a shallow enough angle not to demand more than a 7 or 8 per cent gradient. This should be tame enough over this distance for many to choose between keeping a gently efficient rhythm right to the top, or caning it all the way to Bristol Zoo and collapsing at the finish by the bus stop.

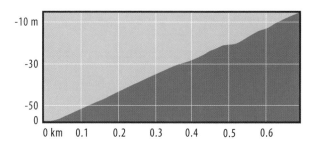

6. BRISTOL HILL

Difficulty	⬤⬤⬤⬤⬤⬤○○○○
Distance	3.7km
Av. Gradient	6%
Max. Gradient	10%
Height Gain	186m
Road Surface	Good
Start Point	North-east Wells. A39 Mountery Road, opposite traffic lights at junction of New Street. GR: ST549461
Local Café	Crofters, Market Place Hotel, 3 Market Place, Wells, Somerset BA5 2RF ☎ 01749 672517

If you wanted to, you could make this a very tough climb indeed. Just getting up it should not be a great challenge, but getting up it fast is quite a different matter. At close on 4km it's one of the longer climbs in this book, but nowhere does the gradient exceed 10 per cent and where it does, the discomfort doesn't last long. No, this hill can take you apart slowly and if you decide to test yourself against the clock you'll need to be aware that you'll have to devote a good ten minutes to pure teeth-gritting pain. It can be a busy road at times, but it's wide and the surface is good and the occasional truck rumbling past is more than made up for by the big views from the epic sweeping bends that the road ahead offers you.

THE CLIMB

At an undemanding 5 per cent, the climb begins steadily enough from the edge of Wells. It's important to keep in mind though that unless you're particularly quick, then you've still probably got well over ten minutes of work ahead of you. And if that thought doesn't dampen any over-enthusiasm, then the steady doubling in gradient to 10 per cent after just 200m surely will. If you look up, ahead and to your left as the fields open out, you'll see the Mendip transmitter mast on the hilltop above you. This is where you're going and as the gradient slackens, you can take the opportunity to establish the pace, as it is here that the hill sets the tone for much of the rest of the climb.

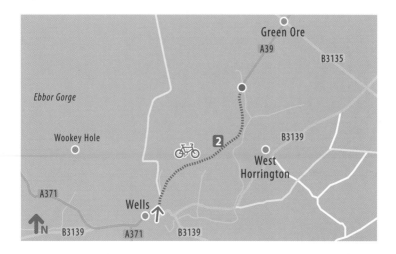

There is another brief kick by the cottage on the bend that takes the gradient back up to a shade below 10 per cent, but it's short-lived. The rest of the climb hovers for the most part between 5 and 7 per cent as the views alternate between wide vistas of Somerset countryside and enclosing stretches of mature woodland. The final couple of hundred metres to

the top rise one last time with a gradient that briefly touches around 9 per cent. After this, the road quickly levels out to finish beside the track to the transmitter mast.

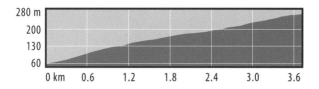

7. BROADOAK HILL

Difficulty	◉◉◉◉◉◉○○○○
Distance	1.7km
Av. Gradient	8%
Max. Gradient	17%
Height Gain	132m
Road Surface	Moderate/Good
Start Point	Queens Road, Bishopsworth, Bristol. At roundabout with junction with Four Acres. GR: ST568677
Local Café	Moondance, 5 South Parade, Chew Magna, Bristol BS40 8SH ☎ 01275 331173

Like its nearby cousin, Winford Lane (Climb 48) on the the other side of Dundry, Broadoak Hill has a bit of an identity crisis. It begins life as Queens Road, down among the suburban streets of north Bristol, an arrow-straight product of 1950s town planning. Then, at an indeterminate point about a third of the way up the north side of mighty Dundry Hill, the road becomes Broadoak Hill, seeming to reflect its transformation from urban residential and shopping street to leafy – if somewhat moth-eaten – country lane. In fact, the road changes its identity a second time as the climb nears the finish, becoming Wells Road at the same time it stops being a hill at all, shortly after the pub.

THE CLIMB

All the work is in the middle on Broadoak Hill. As you pull away from the roundabout the early slope is clear to see rising up at a steady 5 or 6 per cent ahead of you. Don't push too hard here because after about 300m as the trees begin to thicken and the road swings to the left, you'll find the gradient lurches quickly skyward.

Everything changes here. Where moments before, a straight open road on a shallow steady climb gave onto tidy houses, now suddenly the trees close in, low vegetation spills onto the road, the lane twists alarmingly and, most significant of all, the gradient more than doubles in about 200m. By the time you're on the fourth switchback

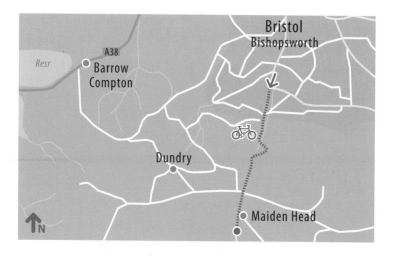

you're working against a 17 per cent slope. This marks the worst of the climbing and from here, the gradient softens to about 10 per cent as it approaches a couple of junctions. Up ahead you'll see a brow and although it's not the top, it does offer a brief rest as a false flat takes you to a last gasp 10 per cent kick to the finish, about 100m beyond the pub and beside a track to the radio mast on your right.

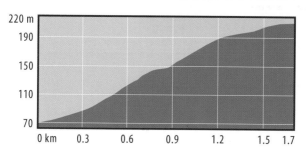

8. BURRINGTON COMBE

Difficulty	◉◉◉◉◉○○○○○
Distance	4.1km
Av. Gradient	5%
Max. Gradient	15%
Height Gain	213m
Road Surface	Good
Start Point	Junction of A368 Bath Road and B3134 The Combe. Approx. 4km west of Churchill Village. GR ST477595
Local Café	The Burrington Inn, Burrington Combe, North Somerset BS40 7AT ☎ 01761 462227

With its early slopes hemmed in by towering limestone cliffs, Burrington Combe is a great looking climb. As you grind your way up, a plaque by a rocky crag to your right claims it to be what gave the Reverend Toplady shelter from a storm in 1775 while he penned his stirring hymn 'Rock of Ages'.

Although Burrington is a long climb, it never gets particularly steep and local road races here usually give riders several laps to gasp their way up it. It is even alleged some stronger competitors are known not to come off their big 52 or 53 chainrings for its entire length. Perhaps something to consider as the kilometres click by.

THE CLIMB

It's not immediately obvious as you leave the junction that you are going uphill at all when you begin this climb. The gradient here starts with a false

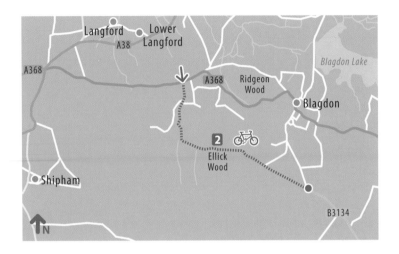

flat, which shortly becomes a shallow climb of around 5–6 per cent. This stays fairly constant past the pub and over the cattle grid and sets the tone for much of the next 2km. Climbing here is steady as you pass between the spectacular rock walls, and remains so until after another 500m when you reach the first of a fairly evenly spaced series of short digs of between 7 and 10 per cent. You will need to allow for these if you want to reach the top in a state of reasonable composure. The last of these short bursts is the steepest, topping out briefly at 10 per cent just before you pass a small parking area on a bend.

As you pass the parking area you'll feel the gradient barely backing off. This is likely to feel uncomfortable after the climbing you've already done, so you'll be relieved to feel the incline reducing as you pass the cattle grid. Unfortunately this is only a temporary reprieve because as you'll see if you look up, there now follows a teeth-clenching heave up a 200-metre incline to the top. This peaks at around 15 per cent. Once over this, a false flat will take you to the top at a junction opposite a farm entrance about 400m further on.

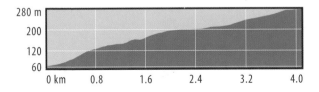

9. CASTLE ROAD

Difficulty	⊙⊙⊙⊙⊙○○○○○
Distance	1.3km
Av. Gradient	9%
Max. Gradient	14%
Height Gain	116m
Road Surface	Good
Start Point	Junction of Castle Road and Bratton Road (B3098). West side of Bratton village. GR ST911522
Local Café	Pickleberry, Fitzroy Farm, Westbury BA13 4RP ☎ 01380 831242

Salisbury Plain remains one of the wildest and most un-spoilt places in Britain. This is largely because a good part of it lies under the control of the MOD and there are consequently very few public roads across it or indeed up onto it. A ride along the bottom of Salisbury Plain's northern edge, however, does yield a few possibilities for the road cyclist looking for a good workout. One of the best of these is probably Castle Road. This takes a fairly direct route to the top of the escarpment via the ramparts of an ancient hill fort from which the lane gets its name.

Although Castle Road is probably not particularly notable for its toughness in terms of length or gradient, it can nevertheless be testing in bad weather. As you emerge from the relative protection of the houses and

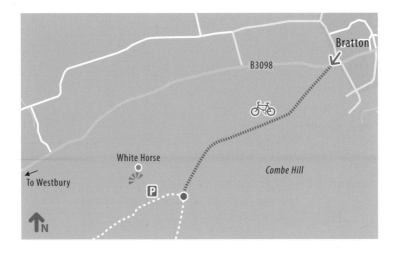

trees on its lower slopes, you may find the exposed nature of this climb towards the top an unwelcome shock just when you least need it.

THE CLIMB

Castle Road begins steadily enough at 6 or 7 per cent for 200 metres past the houses of Bratton. Then, as you emerge from the back of the village, the gradient quickly rises to around 12 per cent before settling down to a little under 10 per cent – a gradient that remains with you for around 700m. Save a bit here as you emerge onto the distinctive grassy landscape of the Plain because the final 50m kicks up again to briefly touch 14 per cent before the road levels out to the finish beside a windswept T-junction. As you regain your breath you might want to take the opportunity to look back and enjoy the view.

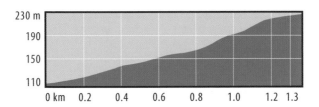

10. CHARLCOMBE LANE

Difficulty	⬤⬤⬤⬤⬤⬤⬤◖○○
Distance	2km
Av. Gradient	9%
Max. Gradient	25%
Height Gain	190m
Road Surface	Moderate
Start Point	Bottom of Charlcombe Lane, Larkhall, 2km north-east of Bath city centre. Bus stop at junction of Spring Lane and Charlcombe Lane. GR: ST758667
Local Café	Emma's Café, 1 Upper Lambridge Street, Larkhall, Bath BA1 6RY ☎ 01225 319257

This climb, nestled at the back of Larkhall on the north-eastern edge of Bath is actually two lanes. Around a third of the way up Charlcombe Lane splits and the climb continues to the top by Colliers Lane. It's the ridge at Lansdown you're making for, dominating Bath's northern skyline, and you'll be climbing it from its eastern side.

THE CLIMB

From the start you can see straight up the steep first 300m of this climb as it strides beside a line of semi-detached houses that step purposefully up the gradient above you. It is here the climb touches 25 per cent before easing back to a more manageable 10 per cent as you leave the buildings below. This easier gradient stays with you for about 400m, occasionally falling to around 7 per cent. Now, you'll need to use this section wisely. Stay composed and concentrate, because ahead the road splits and you'll need to take the right fork. If you're not paying attention here you'll easily find yourself bearing left and careering down the short steep hill that is the continuation of Charlcombe Lane. You don't want to do this: it might feel a blessed relief to your legs, but by this point, you'll not forgive yourself for going the wrong way.

The other reason you'll need this brief softening of the gradient is to grab a chance

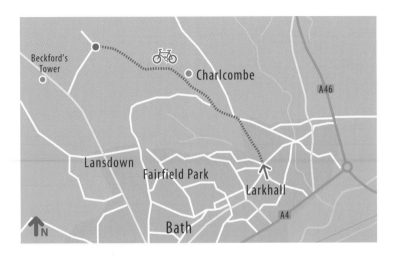

to rest your legs for what's to come. They will still be burning after that steep early section and shortly after the lane divides, the gradient increases again, this time to peak at around 25 per cent as it continues to drive upwards. You're about two thirds of the way now and it is here, by the farm, that the hill slackens off substantially, if briefly, before, in a last 200-metre effort to burst your lungs, the climb turns up finally to the summit, peaking yet again at around 25 per cent before gently touching down on level ground to finish at a sharp left turn by the MOD buildings.

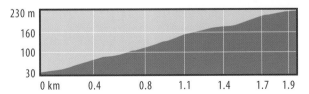

ON CLIMBING HILLS

Since cycling's earliest beginnings, for anybody who spends any time at all getting around by bicycle, the hill has been, at best, a challenge and, at worst, the cyclist's biggest source of dread. From the familiar hill in the middle of the daily commute to the unexpected monster climb at the end of a long day out, hills hold a special place in the heart of any cyclist. Hills are as inevitable to the bicycle rider as the wheels are to their bicycle.

Climbing a difficult hill is, by definition, always going to be a challenge. However, long experience and years of trial and error has taught me a few lessons about getting up them with the minimum of trauma and pain. Simply put, if you can make it less uncomfortable and the experience less intimidating, then you will get up them faster, more comfortably, or both. Dealing with hills effectively is a task that can be broken down into three parts, each requiring a specific approach to the challenge. These are psychological, technical and physical – and all three can be practised and improved.

I have ridden races where the prospect of the approaching climb has sent an audible ripple of misery through the bunch. Riders who are supposed to be there by choice – because bicycle racing is supposed to be fun – are reduced to angst-ridden harbingers of their own doom as what a significant proportion of the riders regard as their personal nemesis looms inexorably above them. But these riders were setting themselves up to suffer even more than they needed and this fact was likely to determine the outcome of their race far more than whether they had any natural ability to climb hills. Confidence in the face of hills is essential, even if, as a poor climber, not physically perfectly built for climbing, you just have reasonable confidence in your ability to limit your losses through technique, strategy and your capacity for recovery when you reach the top. Inevitably, confidence comes with experience. You'll only develop techniques and strategies with practice, so this is one side of the psychology of climbing that needs time to develop.

But there is another more instant psychological trick that is worth trying. It also helps illustrate how easy it can be to fool the mind out of perceived physical discomfort. When I watched Phil Anderson approaching the top of Brassknocker Hill (Climb) in the 1993 edition of the Tour of Britain, he was out of the saddle and tearing his legs to shreds as he hammered his bike towards those few extra points. But despite the pain he must surely have been in, he was smiling – a rictus grin to hide the agony perhaps, but (and I know because I've tried it) also a powerful psychological trick to reduce the negative, resolve-sapping mental effects of pain and muscular exhaustion. Other riders, notably US professional Chris Horner, famous for his smile in the midst of physical adversity, do this too and I suspect all have discovered this old trick. When you're with others, combine this with staying positive and not engaging in the usual mind-altering, gloomy banter about the ter- rible hill approaching and you'll find this will make a surprising difference to your motivation and your perception of the pain you'll experience when the gradient turns up.

Five-times Tour de France winner Bernard Hinault once said a cyclist should be so relaxed when they're climbing that they should be able to play a piano. Aside from the inherent practicalities of lugging a piano up a hill on a bicy- cle, he was making an important point. Remaining as relaxed as possible, despite the physical discomfort you're likely to be in is an important skill that has to be developed and practised. Energy being unnecessarily diverted to muscles to keep them tense, or to shoulders that are rocking unnecessarily, is energy wasted.

Climbing technique is an often underrated skill that can be improved and developed. On steep or very steep gradients, these techniques are particu- larly important to master because they need to be deployed while your body is under a fair degree of physiological stress. When you're moving slowly, your bicycle loses much of its natural stability. You'll find, as the slope increases and your speed decreases, some of your concentration will have to be divert- ed to the task of just staying upright. You are also likely to encounter other difficulties, such as the sudden loss of traction from the rear wheel when out of the saddle. This can bring to a complete stop an already slow-moving bicycle and a wet or muddy road can compound the problem. Add to this gravel, leaves or broken tarmac and the challenge, in addition to that of just keeping the pedals turning, can become considerable. All these factors will need the mastery of some specialist, if simple, riding skills if you are to get to the top of some of these climbs.

While the very low gears that have become popular in recent years can mean, for many, the difference between getting up some of these climbs and not, they can also mean that the extra torque transmitted to the back wheel, combined with the angle of the slope, is likely to cause you to unexpectedly pop a wheelie as you pull on the bars. This is one of the most likely reasons for an inexperienced rider to fall off while climbing because, if you're not expecting it and the gradient is already bringing you close to physical collapse, then there's a good chance you won't be able to react quickly enough to keep the wheel straight when it regains contact. The fall, if it comes, is unlikely to hurt much, but it will mean the end to that ascent attempt. And of course the humiliation you'll feel when you realize you've had a car trailing

up behind you for the last five minutes and is now waiting for you to drag yourself and your bicycle out of its way is not to be underestimated.

All these extra challenges require some practice and experience to overcome. They're not huge, but when they're unexpected and when they come on top of the sheer physical effort of keeping your bicycle going, they can easily be enough to wreck your attempt.

The final factor in getting to the top in a reasonable state – or indeed getting to the top at all – is the most obvious: physical fitness. If you want to get better at it, there is no substitute for riding your bike up hills regularly and often. Not only will this improve your skill and allow you to grow in confidence, it will also make you physically fitter by giving you a more efficient cardiovascular system. This, in physiological terms, is the key component in not just getting you up the hill, but getting you up the hill faster. As well as developing your heart and lungs' ability to get oxygen to your muscles and the waste products away from them, you'll be training the muscle groups responsible for driving you forward, to adapt to the specific requirements of pedalling up hill. Losing excess weight will be another aspect of improved fitness and will be a significant factor in your ability to remain relatively comfortable when climbing steadily, and post a quicker time when you choose to cane it to the top.

These three factors are all dependent on each other – the more you ride, the fitter you get, the more skilled you get and the more confident you get. Then, as your experience develops with all the riding, so the more efficient you get at developing your fitness and the better you'll be at getting up those hills.

Stay with it. As you get used to these very particular challenges of bike riding, like Phil Anderson on Brassknocker Hill in 1993, you'll find you'll be able to deal with them without taking too much attention away from keeping that grin firmly fixed to your face.

11. CHEDDAR GORGE

Difficulty	⦿⦿⦿⦿⦿○○○○○
Distance	3.4km
Av. Gradient	6%
Max. Gradient	19%
Height Gain	165m
Road Surface	Good
Start Point	The Cliffs (B3135), Cheddar. Junction of Cufic Lane, 100m before Cox's Cavern. GR ST466539
Local Café	Derrick's Tea Rooms, The Cliffs, Cheddar, Somerset BS27 3QE ☎ 01380 831242

Its dramatic setting, rising out of the town of Cheddar through limestone cliffs and twisting itself up onto the Mendip Hills is what gives this climb its notoriety. Like its lesser-known nearby cousin Burrington Combe (Climb 8), Cheddar is not a huge challenge, but what it loses in teeth-grinding effort it gains in visual drama. As a popular tourist attraction the gorge is rarely short of sightseers and it may be this that adds to its popularity for those cyclists who never miss an opportunity for a bit of showing off. In 2011 the Gorge's fame as a mecca for cyclists was heightened further when it was included in Stage 6 of the Tour of Britain.

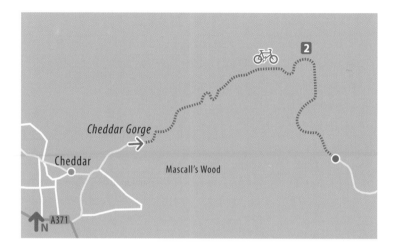

THE CLIMB

Most of the work on this hill comes in the first kilometre. As you leave the gift shops behind, the road quickly rises to around 10 per cent between the cliffs and then, as the climb twists left and then right, the gradient lifts up again to close to 20 per cent. This will hurt, but bear with it because, as the road straightens up, so the gradient falls dramatically. As you leave the rocks and cliffs behind and the trees close in, the riding gets noticeably easier. If they fancy it, stronger riders should find this gradient moderate enough to recover sufficiently from their earlier efforts to really blast up this long drag to the finish. The first kilometre through the trees climbs at around 5 per cent, which then falls to little more than a false flat for the final 500m to the top, ending at a small lay-by on the left.

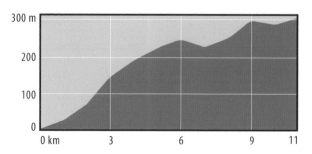

12. CLAVERTON HILL

Difficulty	⬤⬤⬤⬤⬤◯◯◯◯◯
Distance	1.2km
Av. Gradient	10%
Max. Gradient	14%
Height Gain	108m
Road Surface	Moderate/Poor
Start Point	Claverton village, approx. 1.5km east of Bath city centre. Junction with Warminster Road A36 and bottom of Claverton Hill, between the pillars. GR ST789638
Local Café	The Angelfish, Brassknocker Hill, Monkton Combe, Bath BA2 7JD ☎ 01225 723483

OK I admit it, I hadn't done a competitive hill climb for years when – and not entirely for research purposes – I decided to put myself down on the start sheet to ride up this

one properly in anger. Locally, the hill is a well-known climb amongst cyclists and in recent years has become the popular venue for Velo Club Walcot's annual hill climb competition. When I did it I was quickly and very painfully reminded of the difference between riding a bike up a hill in your own time and riding a bike up a hill against the clock.

Towards the top of the hill is the entrance to Claverton Manor, now home to The American Museum, containing artefacts and displays from pre- and post-settlement North American history. In 1897, when it was still a private house, it was the venue for Sir Winston Churchill's first political speech.

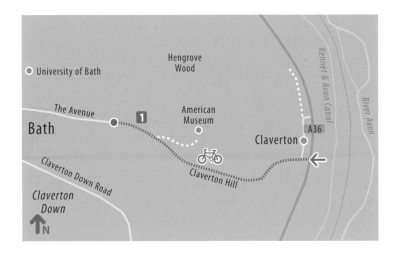

THE CLIMB

This one might be short, but it is fairly brutal. A little after a relaxed start and beyond the village you'll see the lane rear up ahead of you before making off into the trees. As you follow it, you'll feel the gradient getting a grip on your legs as it quickly increases to a little over 10 per cent. After around 250m the slope falls back very slightly and it's here you'll need to settle down because the steady gradient, while staying more or less consistent, will continue to bite chunks out of your thighs for at least the next 500m. Then, with about 200m to go to the museum entrance and when you least need it, you'll feel the slope ramp up again to touch 14 per cent as it jinks left and right ahead of you. This marks the steepest point of the climb and with about 250m left to the top and just when you're wondering how a thousand metres can seem so long, you'll feel the resistance in your legs ease. Finally, as the lane darts away under the trees, you'll pass the finish by a track entrance on your left.

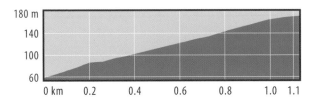

13. CROWCOMBE HILL ROAD

Difficulty	⊙ ⊙ ⊙ ⊙ ⊙ ⊙ ⊙ ⊙ ⊙ ⊙
Distance	1.3km
Av. Gradient	17%
Max. Gradient	26%
Height Gain	191m
Road Surface	Moderate
Start Point	Crowcombe, just off A358. Junction opposite car park entrance. GR ST140366
Local Café	Stable Cottage Tea Rooms, Stable Cottage, Triscombe, Taunton TA4 3HG ☎ 01984 618239

Across the gap between Taunton and the Bristol Channel stretch the Quantock Hills, forming a 24km-long ridge that rises like a great wave from the western end of

the Somerset Levels. The west side is the steepest and this is where Crowcombe Hill Road is to be found. This climb is amongst the fiercest in Somerset: it's not terribly long, but what it loses in distance it certainly makes up for in unremitting steepness.

THE CLIMB

As you enter the lane at the junction, stay relaxed and try to keep your pace even. If you're working too hard at this point you're likely to find yourself in a lot of trouble further up the road. At around 15 per cent the slope is steep, but manageable as you pass the first

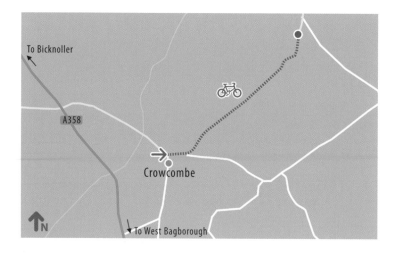

gradient warning sign about 100m from the start. It says the hard bit's still 800m away, but this is optimistic: it's less than half that and by the time you're on it after the first 400m, your legs will already be hurting. Shortly before you get there, much like a condemned man receiving his final meal, you're given a moment where the gradient relents briefly to 9 or 10 per cent. Glean what you can from this respite because, as the lane rises ahead, it's now that the climb really gets to work. For the next kilometre to the top you'll find any fall in the gradient below 20 per cent a relief, with agonizing periods that exceed 25 per cent. The whole experience is made more challenging by the straightness of the road, giving you frequent, unbroken views above you of the climbing still to come.

   The end, when it finally arrives, is marked by a bend about 200m from the top. Dig deep here because, assuming you're still moving, the worst is over. The gradient remains steep, but as you enter the trees, it begins at last to back off, ending in a short, gentle slope to a cattle grid that marks the top.

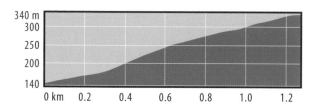

14. DEAD WOMAN'S DITCH

Difficulty	⬤⬤⬤⬤⬤⬤⬤◯◯◯
Distance	2.6km
Av. Gradient	10%
Max. Gradient	20%
Height Gain	160m
Road Surface	Moderate
Start Point	Approx. 1km south-west of Nether Stowey, 200m north of Over Stowey at sharp bend at junction of lanes, close to small tower. GR: ST185387
Local Café	Quantock Tea Room, Nether Stowey, Bridgwater, Somerset TA5 1LN ☎ 01278 732495

Despite its disturbing title, this climb, scaling the eastern slope of the Quantocks, shouldn't render you entirely lifeless as it forces its way up through the woods to the car park on the top. As far as my research could divine, the lane itself has no name, but to be honest, a landmark at the top with a title like that was irresistible. The ditch in question is part of a prehistoric earthwork that got its grim moniker from local eighteenth-century folklore after the body of a murdered woman was found in it in 1789. I last climbed this in late autumn. That day the November mist hung heavy in the gnarled and ancient forest that encloses the lane for most of the climb. As I winched my way up, beneath a tortured canopy of twisted branches, with only my laboured breathing to accompany the patter on wet leaves of a billion tiny water drops, it was hard to ignore the terrible events that gave this place its name.

THE CLIMB

The opening salvo of this climb is gentle enough. At 7 per cent it shouldn't put you into too many difficulties as it takes you the 300m to a sharp left turn that directs you straight up the hillside for the next 2km. From here the slope steadily steepens to 10 per cent as it crosses the cattle grid and, 100m later, touches 20 per cent as you enter the forest. Though uncomfortable, this painful dig is fairly short-lived and the gradient gradually relaxes to a relatively bearable 9 or 10 per cent that will stay with

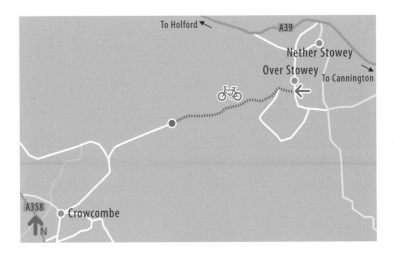

you for most of the next 600m. After that, there is a second leg-grinding section of a little under 20 per cent before once again settling back. Get through this and the worst is over. There follows further steady climbing as you emerge from the trees and soon after, the slope reduces dramatically until a false flat takes you to the finish at a small car park and the nearby landmark that gives this climb its name.

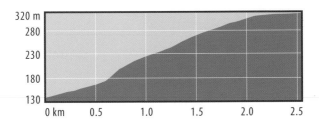

15. DUNDRY LANE

Difficulty	⦿⦿⦿⦿⦿○○○○○
Distance	1.6km
Av. Gradient	8%
Max. Gradient	16%
Height Gain	122m
Road Surface	Good
Start Point	Dundry Lane, junction with A38 Bridgwater Road. Approx. 1.5km west of Bishopsworth, Bristol. GR: ST547679
Local Café	Moondance, 5 South Parade, Chew Magna, Bristol BS40 8SH ☎ 01275 331173

The village of Dundry perches on the very top of Dundry Hill, overlooking the great city of Bristol to the north. Dundry Lane, from the A38 gives the only way up its western flank, with the road taking you directly into Dundry where you'll be finishing the climb just as you enter the village. In November, 1940, 86 people from the city below were given refuge in the village hall after their homes were destroyed by German bombing.

THE CLIMB

The first 800m of Dundry Lane stretches ahead of you, ruler-straight. The gradient is just 6 per

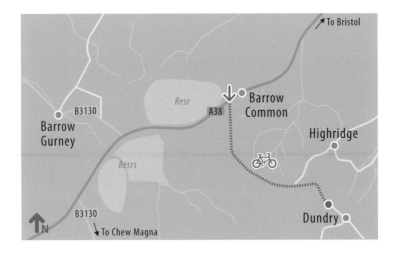

cent here, but it looks more impressive due to the distance you can see up it. From the start, the road ahead will seem to climb high above you as it disappears into a left turn at the trees. As you round this corner and enter the countryside, the character of the climb changes noticeably. Gone, along with the suburban street, is the long view ahead, to be replaced by a more twisting ribbon of tarmac, shrouded by tall hedges. After the bend, the gradient also changes and before you reach the large house on your left, 400m further on, you'll be working against a 16 per cent slope. Just after this, the gradient settles back briefly before kicking again to around 12 per cent up to a junction. Then the going gets easier as St Michael's Church looms over Dundry's rooftops. A final right-hand bend will tell you you're just 200m from the finish. Here the gradient slackens significantly to a short drag before a final 9 per cent kick brings you to the finish at a bus stop just before the wall of a cottage.

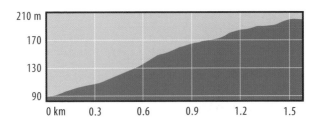

16. DUNKERY BEACON

Difficulty	⊙⊙⊙⊙⊙⊙⊙⊙⊙⊙ ★
Distance	3.3km
Av. Gradient	15%
Max. Gradient	20%
Height Gain	316m
Road Surface	Moderate
Start Point	Junction at bottom of Crookhorn Hill, approx. 600m west of Luccombe and 3km south-east of Porlock. GR: SS906447
Local Café	Horner Tea Gardens, Horner, Porlock TA24 8HY ☎ 01643 862132

Exmoor, tucked in the furthest corner of Somerset, offers cyclists some of the toughest climbing in England and at 520m (1705ft), not only is Dunkery Beacon Somerset's highest point, the road close to its summit is probably its hardest climb.

Beginning in the intricate muddy lanes on Exmoor's northern edge, Dunkery Beacon is an extremely demanding ascent, made even tougher, as you clear the trees, by the exposed nature of the hillside you're grinding up. Behind you the land drops away, open to the north and west, with the Bristol Channel and the mighty Atlantic breathing down your neck. As with all the toughest climbs in this book, steady and calm is best. If, by some miracle, you do have something left after over 3km of excruciating effort, then save it for getting back down.

THE CLIMB

The opening moves of this beast take you up a gently twisting 800-metre grind through the trees of Crookhorn Hill. The gradient on these

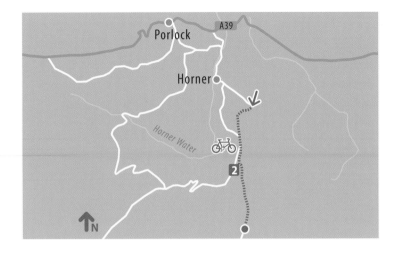

early bends hovers between 17 and 20 per cent before it briefly relents and takes you down a shallow 2 per cent slope. Still in the trees and with 2km still to go, you'll see the road ahead of you rise up as it leaves the protection of the woodland. Here you'll climb gently towards a double switch-back where the gradient kicks up dramatically to around 18 per cent. You'll need to get used to this because, for at least the next kilometre this is where it will stay. Up ahead, stretching away, you'll see a gently snaking ribbon of tarmac going straight up the hillside. This is the long final stretch. From here it's over a kilometre of climbing at around 18 per cent, which, as you near the summit rises briefly to 20 per cent. Once over this you have about 500m to the finish. Only here does the gradient finally begin to fall, first to around 6 per cent and then to a false flat that takes you to the end at the second small car park to your left.

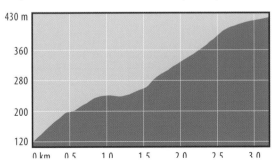

17. EAST DUNDRY ROAD

Difficulty	◉◉◉◉◉◉○○○○
Distance	1km
Av. Gradient	14%
Max. Gradient	24%
Height Gain	104m
Road Surface	Poor
Start Point	Whitchurch, Bristol. Southern end of East Dundry by farm track on right. GR ST600671
Local Café	Moondance, 5 South Parade, Chew Magna, Bristol BS40 8SH ☎ 01275 331173

East Dundry Road, as it wriggles its way up the north-eastern slope of Dundry Hill and out of the ragged edge of South Bristol's suburbs, is a fine example of what happens to an isolated country lane when it's just a bit too close to the corner of a large city. This tiny lane between unkempt hedgerows bears witness through its cracked, shat-

tered and scorched tarmac to traffic volumes beyond its tolerance as well as to its use as an occasional crematorium for stolen cars. The old televisions and broken office furniture on its lower slopes provide further salty urban flavour to this climb as it takes you from the bottom of Bristol to the edge of some of the best landscape and countryside in all of England. At a thousand metres, East Dundry Road is short, but its poor surface and a gradient that spends much of its length in excess of 15 per cent while never falling below 10 per cent until you're within sight of the top means it will give you and your legs plenty to think about.

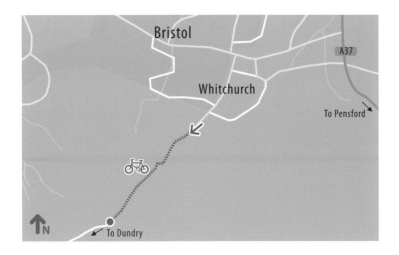

THE CLIMB

Within 200m of starting East Dundry Road you'll find yourself on an 18 per cent gradient as the broken tarmac takes you towards the first sharp bend. Here the slope turns up again, briefly touching close to 25 per cent before dropping back to 18 per cent as you approach the second turn. As you round this, the reduction in gradient to around 15 per cent means you might want to sit back in the saddle to give some different muscle groups a turn with the work. It's a change in rythmn you're likely to need because the lane kicks up again to 20 per cent as you approach the top, reducing to 10 per cent over the brow. This softens again to 8 per cent before finally nearly levelling out to the finish between a pair of field gates to your left and right.

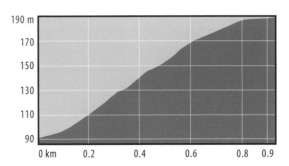

18. EBBOR GORGE

Difficulty	⊙⊙⊙⊙⊙⊙⊙⊙○○
Distance	2.4km
Av. Gradient	9%
Max. Gradient	23%
Height Gain	195m
Road Surface	Moderate
Start Point	By the old charabanc sign, High Street, Wookey Hole. Approx. 30m west of Wookey Hole Caves pedestrian entrance (not the main car park). GR: ST53147
Local Café	André's Café, 84 High Street, Wells BA5 2AJ

Just along from the Old Bristol Road (Climb 32) is Ebbor Gorge, the other southern route up onto the Mendip Hills. Actually, you're not in the gorge, you're in the lane that runs up beside it, which, for most of its length is named Deerleap. As you toil past it, you probably won't see the gorge at all – even though it's close to your right, it is tucked out of sight and buried amongst that gorgeous Mendip landscape. Plenty of interest on this one, with a range of gradients to keep you on your toes as well as in and out of the saddle.

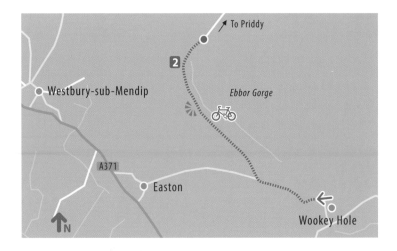

THE CLIMB

For the first 300m nothing much happens as you bump your way up a series of short shallow digs. After that though, things start getting serious. The incline turns abruptly up to around 17 per cent and you're likely to find yourself out of the saddle before the road settles down again to a steady drag. This is a good time to collect yourself before things turn even nastier as you enter the bend ahead. Here, again, the gradient ramps up dramatically to touch 23 per cent. Your legs and lungs will be burning now as it stays steep for another 200m before the climbing backs off to about 7 per cent. Then, as you pass the first car park, the gradient rears up yet again to 15 per cent before briefly levelling out over a series of short bumps as you approach the second car park. It's here the gradient gives you a final 15 per cent dose to bring you to the finish beside a layby at the top.

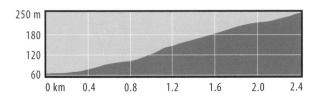

19. GARE HILL

Difficulty	◉◉◉◉◉○○○○○
Distance	1.8km
Av. Gradient	7%
Max. Gradient	14%
Height Gain	125m
Road Surface	Good
Start Point	Beside long track to farm on left, Gare Hill Road. Approx. 3km south-west of Trudoxhill. GR: ST772408
Local Café	The Lighthouse, Tytherington, Frome, Somerset BA11 5BW ☎ 01373 453585

Perhaps even more than its challenge as a climb, what gives Gare Hill its local notoriety is probably its dramatic visual appearance. It soars out of the flat Somerset pasture-land around Trudoxhill before settling gently, a couple of kilometres later, on the wooded northern end of a short ridge.

Because it's a longer climb with several changes in gradient, Gare Hill is a great ride for any cyclist wanting to practise managing their pace. You may also find, if you're a little too quick on the seductively gentler lower half, you'll get an opportunity later on to develop your mental resilience.

THE CLIMB

You're barely aware that Gare Hill has begun as the gradient gently rises from a false flat to a drag before suddenly kicking up, albeit briefly, to around 12 per cent. This can be unpleasant if you've enthusiastically charged up that initial slow rise. From here the gradient settles for a while to a more manageable 5 per cent. Use this as a moment to recover and sort yourself out because after around 400 metres, the gradient will point itself up again. You'll see the church is still high above you, dramatically illustrat-ing the height you still have to reach. Here the gradient increases to 12 per cent and as you round the bend, it turns up again to around 14 per cent. This is the steepest part of the climb.

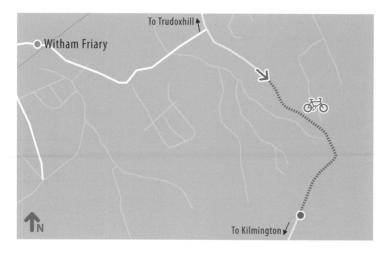

It hasn't finished with you quite yet though. As you clear the bend, you'll be confronted with several hundred metres of wide straight tarmac rising up ahead of you before disappearing over a crest. If you've gone too hard up to the bend this can be a crushing sight. The gradient from here to the far easier final stretch over the top peaks at around 9 per cent and averages about 6 per cent. Not dramatic, but if you've gone too hard up to the bend, you'll feel (and see) every metre of it as you pass the finish beside the entrance to a pair of forest tracks to your left.

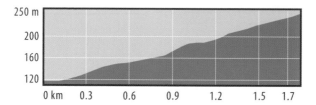

20. GOLD HILL

Difficulty	◉◉◉◉◉○○○○○
Distance	200m
Av. Gradient	17%
Max. Gradient	24%
Height Gain	53m
Road Surface	Cobbles
Start Point	St James's Street, Shaftesbury, at the bottom of Gold Hill, 200m south of Shaftesbury town centre. GR ST862227
Local Café	The Salt Cellar, 2–4 Gold Hill, Shaftesbury SP7 8LY ☎ 01747 851838

The ancient Dorset town of Shaftesbury perches on top of a tall chalk hill and at 219m is one of the highest towns in Britain. With that in mind it's not surprising that Shaftesbury offers at least one excellent climbing opportunity for anyone up for the challenge. In the 1970s, Gold Hill was the location for Ridley Scott's famously evocative Hovis TV ad.

Gold Hill can be a sprint. If your aim is to get up it as fast as you can, then attacking it, teeth bared, trying to ignore the cobbles and out of the saddle straight to the top is probably the best approach. At 200m it's just short enough and most fit riders will have enough in their legs to keep the power on for most or all of the ascent. For everyone else, engaging a suitably low gear and winching their way steadily up can be just as rewarding. Don't take it too slowly though; cobbles have a habit of stopping a slow-moving cyclist dead and on a steep gradient this can mean never managing to get to the top at all.

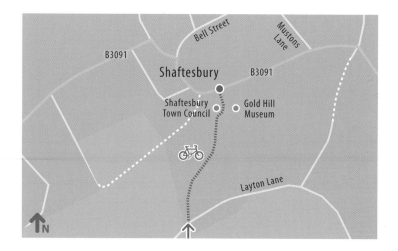

THE CLIMB

As you turn onto Gold Hill you'll see the cobbles don't begin straight away. Here, for a brief moment, the climb on the good tarmac surface remains manageable. That's before the lane disappears around the cottages on the right. As you round this bend you'll see the cobbles beginning up ahead while the gradient quickly increases until, by the halfway point, it's around 20 per cent. Here it backs off slightly for a few metres before rising up again as you make your final kick for the top. The last 20m then presents you with an inexorable, but mercifully brief gradient that begins at around 17 per cent and increases dramatically to 24 per cent. You'll then disappear up the little alley to the left of the restaurant. You'll be in the dark for just a few seconds here before finally finishing on the pavement at the top.

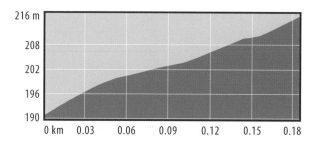

21. HARPTREE HILL

Difficulty	⬤⬤⬤⬤⬤⬤⬤◯◯◯
Distance	1.9km
Av. Gradient	8%
Max. Gradient	20%
Height Gain	148m
Road Surface	Moderate
Start Point	Bottom of Harptree Hill, junction of The Street (A368). Approx. 1km west of West Harptree. GR: ST552568
Local Café	The Stables Tea Room, New Manor Farm, West Harptree, Somerset BS40 6HW ☎ 01761 220172

The villages of East and West Harptree sit close to the bottom of the northern slopes of the Mendip Hills which drop steeply to the flooded valley lakes of Chew and its smaller western neighbour Blagdon. A handful of routes thread their way to the top of the Mendips in this lovely area and all are similarly challenging.

THE CLIMB

Harptree Hill sets off calmly enough for the first 250m. While you won't be particularly tested here, you'll still need to remember to take it easy because, as you approach the first bend ahead, the slope will kick up noticeably to around 15 per cent and as you press on through two further sweeping bends and past a small group of cottages in the trees, this increases again to about 20 per cent. It will hurt here, but the gradient soon reduces to 15 per cent and stays more or less constant right up to the long sweeping bend that beckons ahead of you. Beyond this, the slope reduces dramatically to a long 5 per cent drag that takes you nearly to the finish. If you've worked a little too hard up to this point and you're still reluctant to ease off, this last 500m will be very uncomfortable, particularly as it kicks again briefly just before the top. Grit your teeth now because as you crest this small rise you'll shortly be arriving at the finish beside a layby and two field gates to your right.

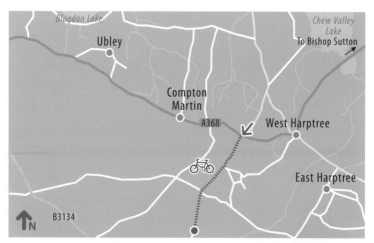

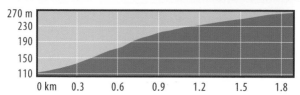

22. HIGH STREET

Difficulty	⬤⬤⬤⬤⬤◯◯◯◯◯
Distance	0.3km
Av. Gradient	16%
Max. Gradient	25%
Height Gain	49m
Road Surface	Moderate/Poor
Start Point	High Street, Woolley, after bridge beside cottage. 400m north-east of village centre; approx. 4km north of Bath. GR: ST750687
Local Café	Emma's Café, 1 Upper Lambridge Street, Larkhall, Bath BA1 6RY ☎ 01225 319257

Two hundred years ago they made gunpowder here. It's hard to believe in this idyllic, emerald valley that the cottages and buildings above you and to the right are the converted and gentrified former factories, stores and offices of the centre of a very profitable local industry that produced gunpowder for export and trade around the world. The Woolley Gunpowder Mill began production in the 1720s and was part of a Bristol-centred network of similar factories throughout the Somerset area. In 1724 tragedy struck the valley when four workers were killed in an explosion that severely

injured two others. Then, ten years later, disaster struck again when another explosion killed Thomas Sandall from the nearby village of Swainswick. Safety procedures presumably improved in the following decades because this was the last serious accident recorded at the mill until its closure in the early nineteenth century.

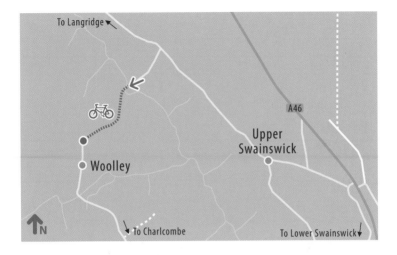

This climb is short, but its glorious setting, combined with its unremitting steepness as it claws its way skyward from the Lam Brook to Woolley village, perched high on a ledge halfway up the valley side, makes it well worth the effort.

THE CLIMB

At over 20 per cent and viewed from beside the cottage at the start, the hectic, twisty first 40m of this hill, all visible before it disappears around the corner above you, is daunting. In case you were considering any other option here, set off steadily because, as you round the bend, the next stretch on a 150m gently sweeping curve to the farm buildings above steepens again to around 25 per cent. You'll really need to dig in here, but the pain is short-lived and, as you pass the barns on the left, the gradient quickly falls to around 15 per cent. After this, though still deceptively steep, the final 100m should pass relatively comfortably to finish at a sharp left-hand corner at the edge of the village.

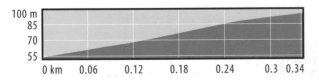

23. HINTON HILL

Difficulty	⬤⬤⬤⬤⬤⬤◯◯◯◯
Distance	1km
Av. Gradient	10%
Max. Gradient	15%
Height Gain	92m
Road Surface	Good
Start Point	Ford Road, bottom of Hinton Hill 1km east of Wellow, layby 20m past the bridge. GR: ST715582
Local Café	Riders' Rest Tea Room, Wellow Trekking Centre, Little Horse Croft Farm, Ford Road, Wellow BA2 8QF ☎ 01225 834376

Once, when I rode this hill in a local hill climb event in the early 1990s I was loaned a bike that a cycle magazine had on test. For its time, the bike was extremely light. In fact, at a touch over 7 kilos, that silk-shod, tubular-tyred titanium beauty would still have compared well to most current top-end machines and, up to then, was probably by far the lightest bike that had ever been up Hinton Hill in bicycling history. Unfor-

tunately we didn't have long to get acquainted. It was hoicked off the roof of the editor's car twenty minutes before I was due to set off and I had to make a quick decision whether to quickly adjust the saddle height and give it a go or whether to stick with my all-steel 9 kilo Bob Jackson road racing machine. Decisions, decisions.... Of course I chose the lightweight

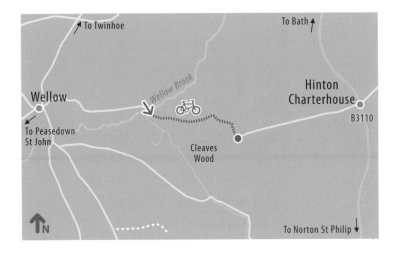

and I swear my unexpectedly high placing that crisp autumn Sunday in 1992 had everything to do with my decision.

THE CLIMB

It's quite clear from the start what you're in for as you reach quickly for the low gears shortly after crossing the bridge. The ridge is obvious above you and the road rises at an ominous 15 per cent to meet it. The slope stays more or less like this for about 500m until the hedges fall away and you approach a short section of crash barrier on the bend. Here the gradient falls to around 10 per cent and after the barrier this slope stays with you for about another 60m. This will take you to the bend above where the gradient finally starts to ease off a little. From here, the climb backs off again to just 6 per cent, reducing in the final metres to a brief drag up to the field entrance on the right that marks the top.

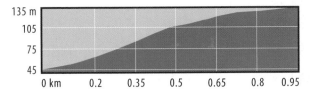

24. HOLT ROAD

Difficulty	⬤⬤⬤⬤⬤○○○○○
Distance	1.5km
Av. Gradient	8%
Max. Gradient	17%
Height Gain	95m
Road Surface	Moderate
Start Point	Holt Road, Second house on left, 60m after right-hand T-junction, approx. 2.5m south-east of Witham Friary. GR ST758383
Local Café	Cat's Café, 23 High Street, Bruton BA10 0AH ☎ 07850 684129

Rising out of undulating Somerset farm and pastureland is a short wooded ridge. To the south lie the magnificent National Trust gardens of Stourhead Park, while to the north, the dusty and self-consciously bohemian market town of Frome. There are a handful of routes to the top of this ridge, but only two that deserve inclusion in this collection. Gare Hill (Climb 19) at the north end marks the highest point of the ridge, but it is probably Holt Road, running up its steep, heavily wooded western side, that takes the prize for the most scenic.

THE CLIMB

For the first 800m of this hill the

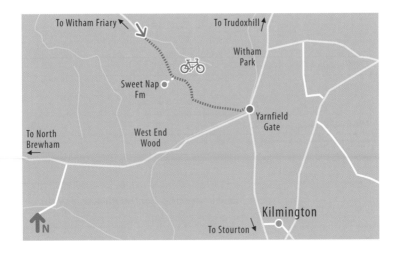

work is undemanding. A steady gradient that varies between 4 and 6 per cent takes you up a gently winding lane into the picturesque woodland that marks the far steeper second half of the climb. As you approach the trees, the road briefly kicks up to around 10 per cent before a sharp left turn takes you into an area of open woodland. Here the gradient settles down to an undulating 5–8 per cent for about 400m until ahead, through the trees, you will see the road turning dramatically up as you approach the tough final 250m of the climb. Here the gradient quickly increases to around 15 per cent as you reach the first of a pair of switchbacks that conclude with a final 17 per cent kick as you near the lodge above you. Push on here because, as the road passes the front of the cottage, the gradient finally softens as you approach the finish at the junction 10m further on.

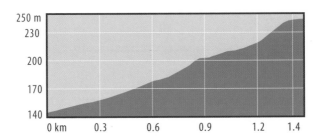

25. LANGRIDGE LANE

Difficulty	⬤ ⬤ ⬤ ⬤ ⬤ ⬤ ◯ ◯ ◯ ◯
Distance	1.9km
Av. Gradient	9%
Max. Gradient	19%
Height Gain	154m
Road Surface	Poor
Start Point	Langridge Lane. Bottom of hollow by small barn after cottages, approx. 700m from junction with Tadwick Lane. Approx. 1km north-east of Upper Swainswick GR: ST715582
Local Café	Emma's Café, 1 Upper Lambridge Street, Larkhall, Bath BA1 6RY ☎ 01225 319257

Langridge Lane bumps and rolls its way up from the bottom of the lovely Swainswick Valley. It's the the most northern of the three big climbs that make their way up the valley's western side to the great ridge of Lansdown on the edge of Bath.

Muddy and treacherous in the wet, this is a restless, undulating climb that requires vigilance as the frequent falls in gradient are often quickly followed by brief, but punishing, returns to tougher climbing just ahead.

THE CLIMB

As you leave the dip beside the barn you'll immediately find yourself on a 14 per cent slope that will take you the 150m to the church. Here, a brief fall in gradient heralds the approach of one of the steepest parts of the climb where the road steadily rises to peak at 18 per cent around 300m after the church. Bear in mind you're only a quarter of the way to the top here, so don't be tempted to attack this steep section too hard. As you reach the left-hand bend, your legs will get another short rest as the gradient backs off again to about 8 per cent before it kicks up to 10 per cent and then drops to a steady 6 per cent for around 200m. As the hedges close in ahead, you'll see the lane steepening as it snakes up towards Langridge. Here again, proceed with caution because, although at 18 per cent, this is the last of the steepest sections, you still

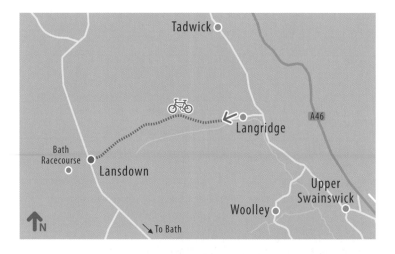

have a kilometre to go. The gradient relents briefly as you pass through the hamlet, only to rear up to 10 per cent as you leave it. This final kick doesn't last long though. With a few hundred metres to go and with its last breath, the climb softens for the final time as 6 per cent becomes a drag, which, for the last 100m, reduces to a false flat to the finish beside a modern building on the right just before the junction.

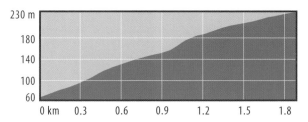

HOW CYCLISTS CONQUERED BRITAIN'S HILLS

It crossed my mind more than once while I was writing this book that every climb listed in these pages must have an unknown name attached to it: that of the first cyclist ever to ride all the way to the top. I also realized, as I sat down to document from the cyclist's eye yet another tiny Somerset lane seemingly going nowhere, that the early un-surfaced condition of these roads meant that most of them were unusable except by foot or on horse-back until at least well into the 1930s.

As well as this, multi-speed gearing on bicycles that was low enough to manage the majority of the climbs listed while allowing the cyclist to ride home again afterwards at something over jogging-pace was not widely available until after the Second World War. The steady developments in bicycle technology over the last century or so and the parallel improvement in British roads since the early years of the last century have made this book possible, giving enough people the means to try for themselves climbs that were, within living memory, impossible even to contemplate on a bicycle.

The push to improve Britain's roads began with the early development not of the car, but of the bicycle. In 1886 the newly established CTC (Cyclists' Touring Club) convened its first Roads Conference, which led to extensive lobbying to improve the usability by cyclists of British roads. The Government listened and over the next forty years Britain's road net-

Campagnolo Gran Sport, the first parallelogram rear derailleur and the design on which all modern rear derailleurs are now based.

Late eighteenth-century advertisement for an early Rover Safety Bicycle. Made by John Kemp Starley in Coventry, it was the world's first commercially successful 'safety bicycle', so named because a rider could put both feet on the floor. 'Far and away the best hill-climber on the market'.

work was transformed from the frequently dilapidated and rutted tracks abandoned by the stagecoaches as people turned to the railways, to the hard, all-weather surfaces that now cover most of our public roads.

But it wasn't only the improvement in surfaces that made British roads and their often precipitous hills manageable by bicycle. Innovations in bike design took the ubiquitous 'ordinary' or 'penny-farthing' of the late nineteenth century and transformed it via John Starley's revolutionary single-speed 'Safety Bicycle' to the lightweight multi-geared road machines most people attempting the hills in this book will be using. Few things can more starkly represent the closing of one technological chapter in the history of the bicycle and the opening of another. A contemporary advertisement for Starley's new bicycle recognized the concerns of most cyclists even then, proclaiming the Rover Safety Bicycle as 'far and away the best hill-climber on the market'.

Hill-climb competitions are as old as cycling, but these races tended to be as much about just getting to the top as they were about winning. In the early days when the 'safety' bicycle was first starting to appear, it was notable how much more successful their riders were over those still determinedly clinging to the old technology embodied in the 'ordinaries' or 'penny-farthings'. Catford CC's archive records an 1887 organized hill climb competition on an un-surfaced road in Kent that saw twenty-four starters. Of those only twelve made it to the top and of them, eight were on the innovative new 'safety' machines, three were on tricycles and just one made it to the top on a penny-farthing.

As the Rover Safety Bicycle continued to develop, innovations in multi-speed gearing further improved the chances of Britain's infamous hills at last being conquered by more than just the super-fit, teeth-gritting specialist on a single-speed bicycle. Although multi-speed gearing was around in various forms from as early as the late nineteenth century it was fairly rare and was not popular with British cyclists. Two developments were to change this. The first took place during the 1930s when the various European racing bodies began to permit mechanical gear shifting in competition, with the 1937 Tour de France seeing it widely deployed for the first time. Then in 1949, Campagnolo introduced the Gran Sport cable-operated parallelogram rear derailleur, a design on which all rear derailleurs have since been based. It was in large part the widespread adoption of reliable gearing based on this design that enabled cyclists in larger numbers than ever before to enter the British countryside on metalled roads that had only a decade or two previously been stony tracks. Furthermore, many hills that had hitherto, even when surfaced, seemed at best an off-putting inconvenience and at worst an impassable barrier, were now frequently manageable.

Since then, while arguably the quality of Britain's rural road network has declined somewhat, bicycles have undergone considerable innovation and improvement. From the dramatic reduction in frame and wheel weights over the last two decades to the widespread introduction of indexed and brake lever-operated gear shifting, as far as cyclists whose interest is never far from their local big climbs are concerned, nearly every one of these innovations has been of benefit.

26. LANSDOWN LANE
(Weston Hill)

Difficulty	⊘⊘⊘⊘⊘⊘⊘○○○
Distance	1.6km
Av. Gradient	11%
Max. Gradient	20%
Height Gain	164m
Road Surface	Good
Start Point	Weston Village, bottom of Lansdown Lane, just after roundabout on Weston High Street 3km north-west of Bath city centre. GR: ST725666
Local Café	The Chelsea Café, 8E Chelsea Road, Bath BA1 3DU ☎ 01225 333688

As you may have noticed by now, the Bath area is peppered with hills. This little beauty strides almost straight up to the precipitous ridge that dominates the city's northern skyline. It is the more brash cousin of Charlcombe Lane (Climb 10) that picks its way more delicately, if a little more challengingly, to the top of the same ridge, but from the other side.

THE CLIMB

The climb begins steadily enough, but as it rounds a couple of early shallow bends the gradient gradually increases from around 5 per cent to a consistent and distinctly uncomfortable 10–12 per cent. The discomfort is not helped by the broadness of the road and the fact that, for the first

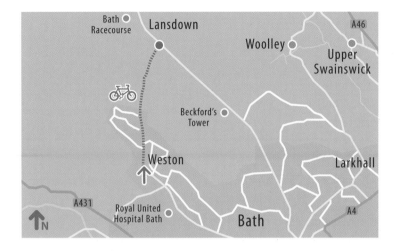

two thirds of the hill, you have a clear, unbroken view of the climb above and ahead of you. Every incremental rise in gradient is clearly visible well before you reach it.

The road steadily steepens and becomes a lane as you clear the houses of Upper Weston. Here the gradient increases again, touching around 17 per cent. This will hurt after the earlier 800m and, as the houses thin out and the hedges close in, it's probably better not to dwell too long on the fact that you're only halfway up.

From here, the road to the top disappears into trees and it is on the bend above you that the gradient takes another kick skyward where it peaks at around 21 per cent. This steep bit might not be for very long, but the previous kilometre of testing gradient will mean your legs and lungs are likely to be at their limit here. The lane continues to jink left and right through the trees for the next 400m, with the slope never falling below 15 per cent. Eventually, as you pass the drive entrance in the trees on your left, the gradient slackens to around 5 per cent. Now you should be able to make out the top up ahead of you. Keep going over the brow to finish at the layby on your right just after the public footpath.

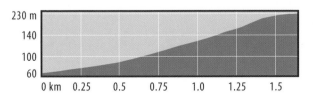

27. LANSDOWN ROAD

Difficulty	⊙⊙⊙⊙⊙⊙○○○○
Distance	2.1km
Av. Gradient	9%
Max. Gradient	16%
Height Gain	184m
Road Surface	Good/Moderate
Start Point	Traffic lights at junction of George Street and Lansdown Road, central Bath. GR ST749652
Local Café	The Adventure Café, 5 Princes Building, George Street, Bath, Somerset BA2 6SG ☎ 01225 723483

In the five or ten minutes it will take to fight your way up this hill you will pass close to some of the most architecturally outstanding buildings in the world.

Setting off from the south-western end of The Paragon, a handsome sweeping Grade I listed Georgian terrace, designed by Thomas Warr Attwood and completed

in 1768, you will shortly pass a second Grade I listed terrace in the road to your right. This is Camden Crescent: ruggedly weathered, with its eastern end swept away in a landslide in 1889. Another 300m further on, you'll pass the entrance to John Palmer's glorious Lansdown Crescent, another Grade I architectural masterpiece. With spectacular views across the city and on a good day, all the way to the Quantocks, sheep are often grazed on the grassy slope in front of the crescent, as they have been for the last two centuries.

There's enough to say about this hill and its neighbourhood to fill a whole book, so I'll stop there and turn my attention to the climb itself.

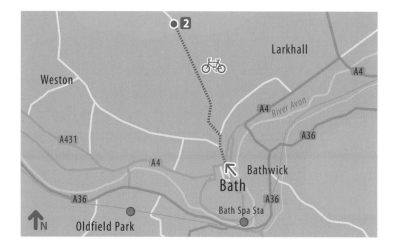

THE CLIMB

Lansdown Road's gradient is remorseless. From the start and for the next 400m you're on a slope of around 10 per cent. Try to keep it steady because this climb is long and from here the gradient increases dramatically as you approach the steepest part of the climb. To the church, 500m ahead, the gradient ramps up mercilessly, peaking at around 16 per cent. Although the slope reduces somewhat as you pass the church, don't forget you're still less than halfway up. The road is now nearly dead straight to the top, with the gradient on the initial part of this final section falling briefly to a welcome 4 or 5 per cent. Unfortunately for those now suffering excessively, it quickly rises again to around 8 per cent before kicking up to around 10 per cent for a short distance. This falls back a little until the final 150m which, in a final excruciating flourish, assaults your smarting legs with a brief 12 per cent slope that takes you to the finish beside the Hare and Hounds across the road to your right.

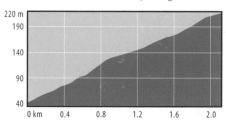

28. MARGARET'S HILL

Difficulty	⬤⬤⬤⬤◐○○○○○
Distance	0.3km
Av. Gradient	18%
Max. Gradient	24%
Height Gain	40m
Road Surface	Moderate/Good
Start Point	Junction of Margaret's Hill and A4 London Road, Walcot, Bath GR: ST751656
Local Café	The Adventure Café, 5 Princes Building, George Street, Bath, Somerset BA2 6SG ☎ 01225 462038

The city of Bath is almost entirely enclosed by a circle of hills. The only two ways out of the city that don't mean at least a fair climb is to brave the busy A4 as it follows the river valley. If you want to stick to the quieter roads then the only way is up and if you want your riding quiet and steep, then the best way out of the city is to head north, through the spectacularly precipitous Camden area. Amongst the several lanes that scale this slope, Margaret's Hill is probably the longest.

Before you set off, look behind you. About 50m down the London Road you'll see St Swithin's Church. The original medieval building that stood there saw the marriage of the parents of the great nineteenth-century author Jane Austen. The churchyard now contains the grave of her father.

If you're able to take your mind off the pain that will surely be wracking your legs as you approach the top of this climb then look to your right. This is Gays House, which until 1829 was a home for destitute girls. It bears a contemporary painted sign that beautifully reflects the values of the time: 'Asylum for Teaching Young Females Household Work'. Quite.

THE CLIMB

Although short, this climb is steep and from the very start, the angle of the street against the houses and walls that enclose it only helps to remind you of this. Quickly

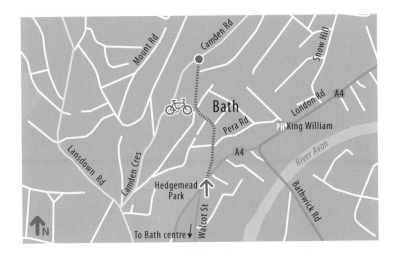

the road rises to well over 15 per cent before kicking up again in places to around 24 per cent as it meanders back and forth. There is no let-up at all on this hill and if it were a lot longer, the final 100m with its clearly visible 20 per cent-plus grind to the top would cause some serious problems. But on this climb, one last big effort should be sufficient to get you to the finish at the junction and level ground.

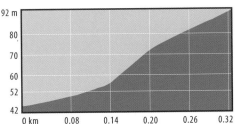

29. MERE HILL

Difficulty	⬤⬤⬤⬤⬤◯◯◯◯◯
Distance	1.2km
Av. Gradient	9%
Max. Gradient	16%
Height Gain	111m
Road Surface	Moderate
Start Point	B3095 east side of Mere, just after the bridge. GR: ST817328
Local Café	Angel Corner Tea Rooms, Angel Lane, Mere, Wiltshire BA12 6DH ☎ 01747 860524

This is a climb that always causes me problems. It shouldn't be that hard, but whenever I'm on it I find I'm suffering badly before I'm even halfway up. Maybe it's the easy, long and gentle downhill through Mere prior to the climb that catches me out and tricks me into overdoing the early pace. Perhaps it's the two hard digs that rear up at regular intervals further on up the road that I consistently underestimate. Whatever it is, when I finally drag myself onto the pristine downland at the top, I always feel a sense of relief out of proportion to that which any sombre analysis of this hill is ever likely to provide.

THE CLIMB

The start of Mere Hill is nicely defined. From a flat beginning under the A303 it curves up and away from you almost immediately before disappearing around a bend about 100m ahead. Steady here: the gradient quickly peaks at 13 per cent once it's out of sight and from there you'll get precious little respite until you're nearly at the top which, remember, is still a kilometre away. In about 200m you'll get a brief rest when the gradient settles back to a more reasonable 6 or 7 per cent. Use this 200–300 metres to regain some composure. The landscape now opens out on your right and the ribbon of road, snaking first right then left, reveals itself almost in full before disappearing again behind some trees in the distance. Here you'll start to feel the resistance in your legs growing again as you near the steepest part of the climb. The gradient

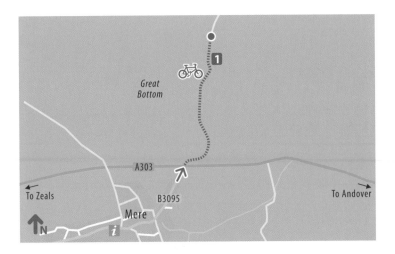

now increases inexorably as you approach and round the final bend, where it peaks at around 16 per cent.

Although you're now through the steep stuff, there follows a wince-inducing, 200-metre, straight line grind to the top, which levels out only painfully slowly to finish on a false flat beside a farm gate on the left.

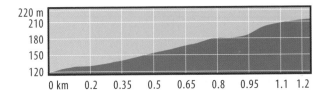

30. NEW ROAD

Difficulty	◎◎◎◎◎◎◎◎◎◎
Distance	1.8km
Av. Gradient	13%
Max. Gradient	25%
Height Gain	221m
Road Surface	Good
Start Point	Draycott. Junction of New Road and A371, approx. 2km south-east of Cheddar. GR ST476511
Local Café	Stable Cottage Tea Rooms, Stable Cottage, Triscombe, Taunton TA4 3HG ☎ 01984 618239

'You're not gonna ride up that are you?' was my unexpected introduction to this lesser-known Mendip beast. The old local man with the heavy Mendip accent was

walking past with his Jack Russell when he spotted me sorting myself out at the bottom of the climb, preparing for the ascent. His incredulous tone was not misplaced. This is regarded as the hardest climb on the Mendip Hills. Not only is it consistently steep for much of its length, but, because it runs almost straight up the hillside to the top, you are forced to endure the mental torture of being able to see most of what's ahead of you as you're still struggling up it. For many, the psychological effect of this cruel visual trick can often be the deciding factor on whether a rider finally cracks, does the unthinkable and climbs wearily off.

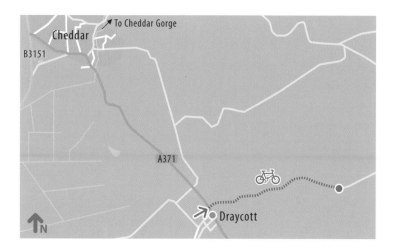

THE CLIMB

There's no let-up here. No gently rising gradient to warm you into it, no intermediate brief flatter bit. Not even the visual distraction of a corner or two. From the start, the gradient quickly rises to 10–15 per cent and after 200m it just gets steeper, gently pointing you up to around 20 per cent for another few hundred metres. This then rises again to 25 per cent, a gradient that stays with you more or less for the next 300m. This is a testing stretch, but if you can drag your eyes away for a moment from the patch of tarmac just ahead of your weaving front wheel and look up, you'll see a brow in the road. It's not the top, but it does mark the end of this very steep section. Once you're over this, the 10–15 per cent slope you're now on will make your legs think they're enjoying a rest. This continues for a few hundred metres before falling to 7 per cent and then petering out to a welcome drag to the finish at a gate on the right, shortly after the airfield.

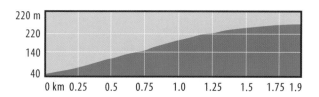

31. NEWTOWN

Difficulty	⦿⦿⦿⦿⦿⦿○○○○
Distance	2.3km
Av. Gradient	7%
Max. Gradient	17%
Height Gain	140m
Road Surface	Moderate
Start Point	Junction of Newtown and Bratton Road (B3098), Westbury. GR: ST876513
Local Café	Pickleberry, Fitzroy Farm, Westbury BA13 4RP ☎ 01380 831242

Newtown and its wilder but shorter neighbour Castle Road (Climb 9), 5km to the east, are probably the two toughest road climbs you'll find to take you onto Salisbury Plain. Despite this, neither offers an enormous physical challenge, although on a clear day you'll be well compensated for this lack when you find yourself able to look up from your labours from time to time to glimpse the tremendous views that feature on both these climbs. As a bonus, Newtown also includes various dramatic views of the nearby Westbury White Horse.

THE CLIMB

Newtown quickly sets about you with a vengeance. From the start, straight as an arrow for around 200m, the road climbs purposefully at 12 per cent. Bear with this because the discomfort you'll be in is only temporary. As you clear the rise, a drop in gradient to around 4 per cent will give you a brief rest before the road starts to climb again as the fields open out to the White Horse on your left. In another 400m, the cottage on the bend tells you you're nearly halfway up the climb. Unfortunately it also tells you the real hard work is about to begin.

As you pass the house and enter the trees, the gradient quickly doubles to around 10 per cent. This falls back again briefly before steadily increasing through 12 per cent, past 15 per cent, to peak momentarily at 17 per cent before falling again to 12 per cent as the trees thin and the hillside tumbles away to your left. Another

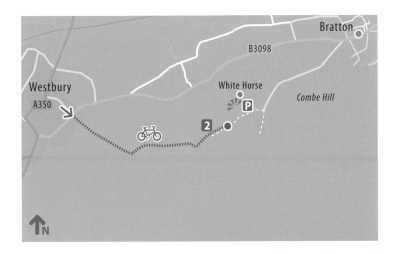

fall in the gradient here to single figures should allow you to gather yourself sufficiently to deal with this climb's last effort to finish you off. The next 150m touches 15 per cent before it reaches the bend and it is here the hardest work ends. It's not quite done with you yet though. Press on to follow the contour lines to the top. You still have

another 500m to go, but the road levels significantly now you've made the ridge. A false flat will take you the finish beside the Jubilee Beacon on your right.

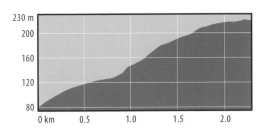

32. OLD BRISTOL ROAD

Difficulty	◎◎◎◎◎◎◎○○○
Distance	3.2km
Av. Gradient	6%
Max. Gradient	17%
Height Gain	181m
Road Surface	Good
Start Point	Junction of Old Bristol Road and Ash Lane, 50m north-west of junction with Bristol Hill A39. Approx. 1km north of Wells city centre. GR: ST549464
Local Café	Crofters, Market Place Hotel, 3 Market Place, Wells, Somerset BA5 2RF ☎ 01749 672517

The Old Bristol Road was the scene of British rider Jonathan Tiernan-Locke's King of the Mountain victory in Stage 6 of the 2011 Tour of Britain. It's still one of the tougher climbs on the Mendips and although it's fairly long as Somerset climbs go, much of the sting is removed on its early slopes when the road takes you on a brief downhill meander through Upper Milton.

THE CLIMB

You'll find yourself beginning this climb with only moderate effort for the first 300m. Then, as the lane rounds the first of two sharp bends the lane turns dramatically up to around 17 per cent. The discomfort is only brief, however, and before you know it you're on a short but welcome descent through the hamlet of Upper Milton. While this represents only a momentary opportunity to clear some of that lactic acid, it still makes a fair bit of difference to the state of your legs – and your mind – as the road turns up again by the farm. From here and for the next 800m the gradient remains at a steady 5–7 per cent and even, for a moment, nearly levelling as you pass the crash barrier in the trees.

Now, if you've been hammering the pace up to this point, throwing caution to the wind and indulging yourself in the moderate incline of the last kilometre, then you may

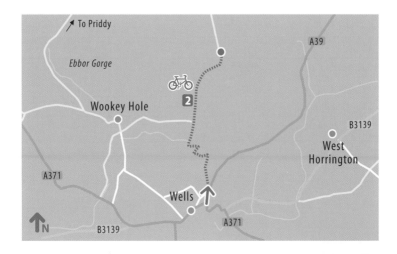

find the final 800m to the top of this hill a challenge. From this point to the summit, the road adopts an almost unremitting 17 per cent gradient. As you emerge from the trees with 400m to go, your legs and lungs burning, look to your right. Above you across the fields towers the 91-metre Mendip Transmitter, the base of which stands level with the height you still have to achieve. Keep going, because ahead you'll see the road bending to the left and it's beyond there that the gradient finally and quite suddenly eases to a false flat for about 50m to where the climb ends beside a farm track to your right.

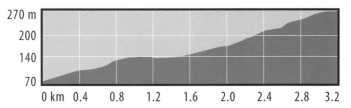

33. PARK HILL

Difficulty	⬤⬤⬤⬤⬤◯◯◯◯◯
Distance	1.8km
Av. Gradient	7%
Max. Gradient	14%
Height Gain	132m
Road Surface	Excellent
Start Point	Longleat Park main entrance road, 200m east of the house front at the cattle grid by the boating lake. GR ST810428
Local Café	Bargate Cottage Tea Rooms, Bargate Cottage, Shearwater, Wiltshire BA12 8AE ☎ 01985 215153

This has got to be the best manicured climb in the country. Nearly 2km of immaculate tarmac, snaking up a pristine Capability Brown hillside – every tree, hummock, water pool and thicket thoughtfully chosen and placed by the great landscape artist himself

to build a vast and harmonious scene of rural English tranquility. Not that you'll be noticing, much less thinking about any of that as you winch yourself up the slope from the front of one of England's most famous Elizabethan stately homes.

As you make the ascent of Park Hill, you may notice several animals grazing in the park below not commonly seen in the Wiltshire countryside. So, if you thought you saw a rhinoceros through the trees on the Wiltshire veldt below, this is not an hallucination brought on by the agony of hitting the second part of the climb too hard; this will in fact be a rhinoceros.

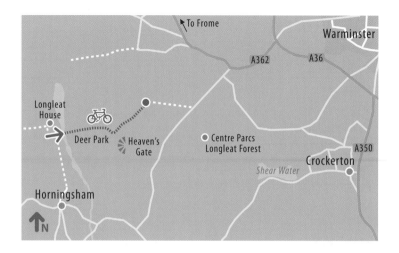

THE CLIMB

Park Hill gets down to business almost from the start, easing you in with a moderate gradient of around 5 per cent. This then briefly kicks up after a few hundred metres to a little under 10 per cent to a second cattle grid. It's then about 300m at 7 or 8 per cent to a sharp left-hand bend. This points you across the side of the hill in a straight line, just shy of a kilometre to the top. From the bend, if you can take your eyes off the grazing rhinos for a second, you can see straight up the road as it pitches and rears its way above you to the top. This is the toughest section. If you took off too quickly at the bottom then you're likely to find the next few minutes or so an ordeal as the gradient quickly increases from about 7 per cent at the bend, past 10 per cent, up through 12 per cent, to peak finally at 14 per cent. The finish is about 40m before the cattle grid.

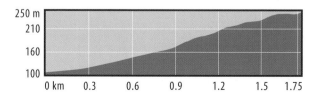

34. PARK STREET

Difficulty	⬤⬤⬤◍○○○○○○
Distance	400m (437 yards)
Av. Gradient	6%
Max. Gradient	10%
Road Surface	Good
Start Point	Pedestrian crossing at the bottom of Park Street (A4081), Bristol. Close to junction of Unity Street. GR: ST583728
Local Café	Mud Dock, 40 The Grove, Bristol BS1 4RB ☎ 01179 349734

Park Street could be said to be the beating heart of Bristol. At the bottom sits College Green: a tiny, but perfectly formed public park spread in front of the Grade II-listed City Hall and seat of Bristol's local government, completed in 1956 after the Second World War interrupted its construction. At the top of the hill is the Wills Memorial

Building, now an annexe of Bristol University. Designed by Sir George Oatley and opened in 1925, it is the last major Gothic building to be constructed in Britain. Like City Hall, it is also Grade II-listed.

Park Street stretches between these two structures. Grandly broad and pencil-straight, it was begun in 1761 and is Bristol's oldest example of a uniform, stepped terrace. On 24 November 1940 the same German bombing raid that drove some of Bristol's residents to the top of Dundry Hill (Climb 15) destroyed or badly damaged about a third of Park Street, most of which was restored after the war.

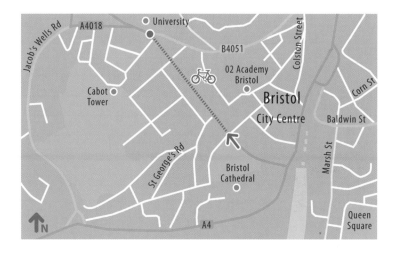

The hill has also been the occasional venue for the dramatic, noisy and highly entertaining night time 'Red Bull Hill Chasers' hill climb competition, an open hill climb event (very open!) which is like a normal club hill climb competition, but raced in pairs and very definitely without the tea urn.

One last thing before you start: just as you set off, look to your right. On the wall set back is a famous Banksy mural – the one of the naked man hanging out of the window.

THE CLIMB

This is probably the longest climb in the book where you can see the top from the bottom. You'll set off from the lights on what is more or less a flat piece of tarmac, but very quickly the road ramps up to around 7 or 8 per cent. Here it will stay for the next 200–300 metres. There is a brief moment where the gradient exceeds 9 per cent, but by then you'll be well within sight of the traffic lights at the junction that marks the top.

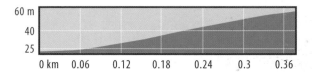

35. PORLOCK HILL

Difficulty	⊙⊙⊙⊙⊙⊙⊙⊙⊙ ★
Distance	3.9km
Av. Gradient	14%
Max. Gradient	25%
Height Gain	356m
Road Surface	Good
Start Point	Outside The Ship Inn, High Street (A39), Porlock, Somerset. GR: SS884467
Local Café	The Ship Inn, High Street, Porlock, Somerset TA24 8QD ☎ 01643 862507

This hill is legendary. And not just amongst cyclists; there are scores of motorists too, who, over the last century, have found themselves at Fate's mercy when their sizzling brakes have finally expired on the horrendous 25 per cent double switch-back towards the bottom of this monster. All will bear testimony to both the length and the steepness of this hill.

For cyclists going up it, the problems are straightforward: the length, combined with the gradient. This is a psychological test as much as anything because once the steepest section is eventually done with destroying your legs, the climb continues with only the briefest of respites, if in more modest spirit, right to the top. No, this climb is not for the faint-hearted. The glorious views across Exmoor and to Porlock Bay far below are likely to stay un-witnessed as you fight just to survive this challenge.

THE CLIMB

From the inn, the climb snakes ominously

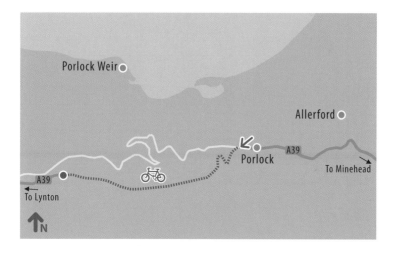

ahead at around 12 per cent. Remain absolutely steady and focused here because, as you approach the first hairpin after 400metres, the gradient lurches up to 25 per cent and this is where it will stay, around the next bend and all the way up to the second hairpin, 300m ahead. After this, the climb backs off a little, falling to around 20 per cent up to the fourth bend. The slope then drops again to 10 per cent and then briefly to 6 per cent. This point, nearly a kilometre from the start, marks the first time the gradient falls below double figures. Try to find a quiet place in your mind now and stay there because the gradient soon rises again to 15 per cent as the moorland opens out and you cross the cattle grid. Ahead there's a crest, but be warned: this is *not* the top. Press on over it to a short, but very welcome, 2 per cent downhill that will take you to the final part of the climb. Now on exposed open moorland, this descent will quickly become a 3 per cent drag, which will turn into, as you approach the top, a 12 per cent climb and the scene of the final battle. When you get yourself up this, you're done.

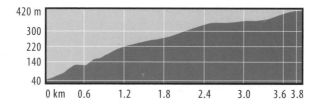

36. PORLOCK TOLL ROAD (New Road)

Difficulty	◎◎◎◎◎○○○○○
Distance	6.8km
Av. Gradient	6%
Max. Gradient	8%
Height Gain	382m
Road Surface	Moderate/Good
Start Point	Outside Porlock Village Hall. Junction of New Road and High Street (A39), Porlock. GR: SS883467
Local Café	Whortleberry Tearoom, High Street, Porlock, Somerset TA24 8PY ☎ 01643 862891

Around 1840 the Porlock Manor Estate built a toll road to give travellers in carriages not wanting to risk the brutal Porlock Hill (Climb 35) a fighting chance of getting onto Exmoor. Then, with the development of the motor car, more and more travellers, unable to get their new-fangled contraptions up or safely down the old road, turned left at the top or took the right fork at the bottom to clatter and bang their way up this far more scenic 7-kilometre detour instead.

While by far the longest climb in the book, nowhere does the gradient exceed 8 per cent, mostly ticking away at a steady 5–6 per cent. You can charge up this one for a fast time if you want, but it's equally rewarding to stay in the saddle and soak up the glorious woodland scenery that will grace most of your journey to the spectacular vis-

tas at the top. Perhaps not the main reason why the riders in the Tour of Britain came up here for Stage 2 in 2007, but a far better prospect than the leg-busting alternative just a couple of hundred metres south.

This is still a private road and despite the estate's slightly mean-spirited insistence on charging cyclists to use it, it's well worth the ride.

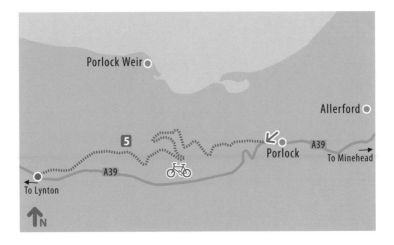

Don't say I said it, but if you're quick enough, you might just flash by the toll booth without them noticing you.

THE CLIMB

The first few hundred metres of this climb set the tone for the next 6km. A steady gradient of 5–6 per cent works its way along the contours of the hillside with only the occasional hairpin a not unwelcome interruption to your rhythm. Now and again the slope gives your legs a gentle poke as it tips up to 8 per cent, but otherwise you're left alone to enjoy the ride. At around 4km the trees will thin and as you cross a cattle grid, the glorious views across the Bristol Channel will open out for you. Push on for the next 3km across the moor, still gently climbing, until you reach the junction that marks the finish.

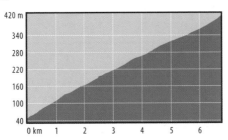

37. PROSPECT PLACE

Difficulty	○○○○○○○○○
Distance	0.7km
Av. Gradient	17%
Max. Gradient	30%
Height Gain	95m
Road Surface	Moderate
Start Point	Bathford Village approx. 9km north-west of Bath. Junction of High Street and Prospect Place. GR: ST796666
Local Café	The Raft Café Boat, Tyning Road, Bathampton, Bath BA2 6TQ ☎ 017733 336989

Doubtless like many others, the first time I rode Prospect Place many years ago, I was soundly beaten by the utterly spirit-crushing sight that greets nearly everyone attempting to ride up it for the first time: when you reach the sharp bend and you look

up, you will see that, far from any soften-ing of the murderous gradient, the hill, as it disappears into the trees, actually and quite clearly gets even steeper.

If you approach this hill from the west, you'll have a fair climb just to get to the bottom of this little beauty. I had consid-ered including in the challenge this initial approach up Bathford Hill, but I thought because this would mean turning right into Prospect Place on an at times fairly busy road, this would not be in the spirit of the book. Of course, if you feel like you're up for it, have a go from the main road down in the valley. Remember though, it will mean an extra kilometre of climbing even before turning right into Prospect Place for the final brutal assault.

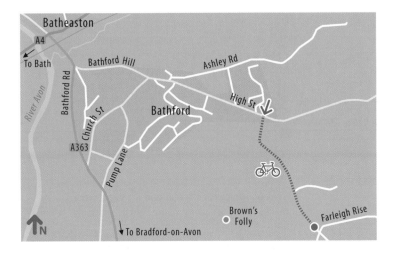

THE CLIMB

This little beast begins immediately, heading straight up between houses at a consistent gradient of at least 22 per cent before disappearing around a sharp left turn. It's absolutely essential you don't attack this early section too hard.

From the notorious bend, you're in plus-25 per cent territory and even though it may not feel like it, it is here you'll be cashing in the care you took on the first 150m. You now have nearly half a kilometre of climbing that never falls below 22 per cent and briefly touches 30 per cent. 200m ahead you'll see a false summit. Here the gradient lessens to something that is relatively less steep, the slope settling at a little under 20 per cent. But it is only in the last 100m that the climb properly relents and you're left to spin your shattered legs along a false flat to a stop about 30m before the bus shelter on the corner.

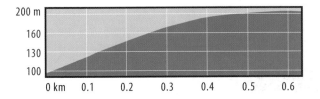

38. ROSEMARY LANE

Difficulty	◉◉◉◉◉◐○○○○
Distance	0.7km
Av. Gradient	12%
Max. Gradient	23%
Height Gain	64m
Road Surface	Moderate/Poor
Start Point	Rosemary Lane. Western end of bridge by the old Freshford Mill, Sharpstone, nr. Freshford. Approx. 4km south-east of Bath. GR: ST785596
Local Café	The Galleries Café, Freshford Lane, Freshford, Bath, Somerset BA2 7UR ☎ 01225 723249

The lovely village of Freshford sits tucked in and on the slopes of a forested valley just off the A36. Any cyclists finding themselves here, however, will quickly discover its dark side. Once they have become entangled in Freshford's labyrinth of streets and lanes, the only way out is up one of a small handful of painfully steep climbs of which the benign-sounding Rosemary Lane, the main street of the associated hamlet of Sharpstone, is the steepest.

This short but fairly cruel ascent begins on a tired old bridge over a broad and lazy stretch of the River Frome. To your left is the now disused Freshford Mill, its picturesque location and seventeenth-century heritage giving no clue that it produced car parts until 1993. At the time of writing the site is being developed for housing, which seems sad, as this is a beautiful and very peaceful corner of a delightful and intimate little valley. It seems hard to imagine as I look across to the bland walls of new, bright white stone – chosen as a nod to the vernacular – that the area won't be ruined for ever.

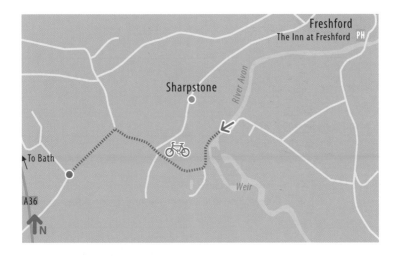

THE CLIMB

For the first 150m of this climb, an easy slope of around 5 per cent will take you round a gentle bend. This will point you up the very tough 200-metre section of the climb. Sharpstone clings to the side of a steep slope, 23 per cent in places, and as you winch your way up between the houses you'll feel every metre of it. The gradient relents now and again, dropping back at times to around 15 per cent and this will feel like a relief, but only before the slope begins to rise again. With 200m to go, once you've reached the junction, the hard stuff finally backs off significantly. But it's not quite over yet. Keep going through the junction, turning left. Here the gradient falls to 10 per cent, which eases again to 6 per cent. This will take you at last to the finish by the hotel entrance on your right and the playing field to your left.

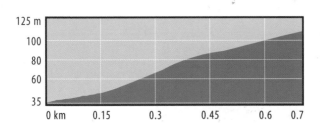

39. SHAFT ROAD

Difficulty	⬤⬤⬤⬤⬤⬤⬤◯◯◯
Distance	1.3km
Av. Gradient	8%
Max. Gradient	20%
Height Gain	102m
Road Surface	Moderate
Start Point	30m along Shaft Road from junction with Church Lane, Monkton Combe. Approx. 4km south-east of Bath. GR: ST774621
Local Café	The Angelfish, Brassknocker Hill, Monkton Combe, Bath, Somerset BA2 7JD ☎ 01225 723483

Just along the lane from Brassknocker Hill (Climb 4) sits the less well-known Shaft

Road. It ascends the same ridge as its more famous cousin, but is often missed by cyclists because it lies away from the main road, buried amongst the hedges and cottages of Monkton Combe. It's probably for this reason that Shaft Road doesn't enjoy the same illustrious history of visits by some of cycle sport's greatest legends. This is a shame because as a climb, Shaft Road offers not only a challenge that is almost as tough as Brassknocker, but one that is probably more interesting. From the oddly rural Victorian suburban street setting at its start, to the trendily tatty hamlet clinging to the slope further up and with its multiple changes in gradient, Shaft Road has plenty to offer.

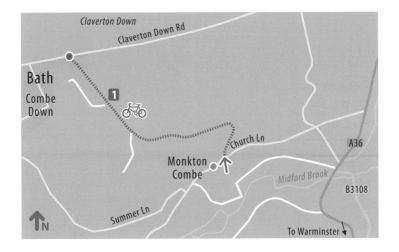

THE CLIMB

This hill begins calmly enough. Between clipped hedges, the lane swings slowly left on a gradient that gently ramps up to around 7 per cent. As the bend continues round, so the gradient continues increasing until it briefly touches 20 per cent, which then reduces over the next 200m to just 5 per cent. This is good. It will give you a brief chance to recover, because, as you approach the cottages and as the road begins to twist back and forth above you, the slope rises up again, hovering at a shade below 20 per cent for the next 100m. To your left the landscape opens up to glorious views as the gradient once again softens perhaps just enough for you to steal a look.

For the next 200m the slope keeps up a consistent 10–13 per cent until it gives you one final brief kick before at last slackening off to a drag that takes you the last 300m to the top, about 40m before the junction at the end of the lane.

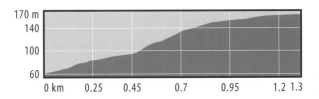

40. SHIPHAM ROAD

Difficulty	⬤⬤⬤⬤⬤⬤⬤◯◯◯
Distance	1.8km
Av. Gradient	9%
Max. Gradient	17%
Height Gain	140m
Road Surface	Good
Start Point	Shipham Road 150m north of Junction of A371 and B3135 Axbridge Road. Approx. 0.5km north-west of Cheddar. GR: ST449546
Local Café	Lillypool Café and Farm Shop, Shipham Road, Cheddar, Somerset BS25 1RQ ☎ 01934 741244

The north-west corner of the Mendip Hills offers several routes to the top and while Shipham Road is perhaps the least picturesque of a very good bunch, it remains a fairly demanding hill that does give the rider an opportunity to test themselves on a reasonably long climb with a consistent, if not brutally testing gradient. Climbing Shipham is a steady, drawn out process with very few opportunities for a change of pace or rhythm.

THE CLIMB

Shipham Road is a wide, sweeping climb that begins by quickly ramping up to around 11 per cent. The gradient doesn't get a great deal steeper than this for the next 1.5km, but then again, it doesn't get a lot easier either. From the very start there's plenty of time to contemplate the steadily climbing road ahead, with few bends to obscure the road as it threads its way up ahead of you.

From that initial 400m, the gradient increases again, with occasional digs of 16 or 17 per cent. The climb continues in this manner all the way to the second quarry entrance, some 1.3km further on. Here the road levels out to a false flat for 200 metres or so, where you can gather yourself – even shift into a bigger gear maybe – confident that there is just one final and brief 7 per cent heave to the top. After this, the climb gently peters out to its end at a small grassy layby just beyond the quarry sign.

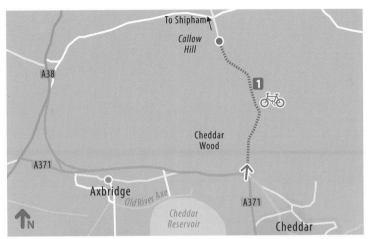

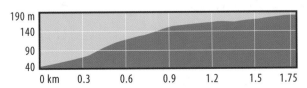

41. SMITHAM HILL

Difficulty	◉◉◉◉◉◉◉○○○
Distance	2.8km
Av. Gradient	9%
Max. Gradient	17%
Height Gain	179m
Road Surface	Moderate
Start Point	East Harptree village, junction of Middle Street and Whitecross Road. GR: ST567559
Local Café	The Stables Tea Room, New Manor Farm, West Harptree, Somerset BS40 6HW ☎ 01761 220172

The lane you'll be riding up is actually called Middle Street. Smitham Hill in fact refers to the topographic feature whose northern flank you'll be scaling. At the top, across the fields and beyond the trees to your right is the Grade II-listed Smitham Chimney,

a nineteenth-century relic from the area's past as a centre for lead production. The ground all around now contains high levels of lead contamination and as a result supports a very rare population of Ditrichum plumbicola, a species of tiny moss that thrives on lead spoil. Every cloud has a silver lining, I suppose.

THE CLIMB

This climb teases and teases. When you set off, you're quickly put to work on a 15 per cent gradient, which, after just a couple of hundred metres eases off as the houses start to thin out, fall-

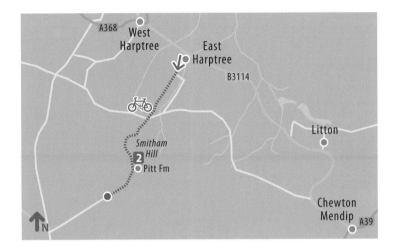

ing to just 7 per cent. Then, with 500m done and just as you're settling in for some steady climbing, the slope drops again to little more than a moderate drag, followed by a quick rise before yet another drag brings you to a steeper section which backs off yet again up to a cottage on a bend. It is only here the harder stuff gets going. If complacency had set in for the first 1200m of this climb and you've been a bit too energetic, then now is the time that regrets may be setting in. The road lifts quickly on the bend to 17 per cent, which stays with you for about 300m up to a group of cottages. The slope backs off a little here and then drops away again to a brief false flat between hedges where ahead you'll be able to see the lane turning upwards towards the trees. As you pass the farm on your left and enter the woods, the hard work starts again, with the gradient touching 15 per cent before you're out of the trees. As you leave the wood, the slope reduces, diminishing to another brief drag that then becomes another kick of about 7 per cent to the brow that you can see ahead of you. The finish is by a field gate on your right, 200 metres or so further on.

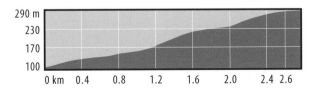

42. STEWAY LANE

Difficulty	⬤⬤⬤⬤⬤⬤⬤◯◯◯
Distance	1.8km
Av. Gradient	9%
Max. Gradient	25%
Height Gain	148m
Road Surface	Poor
Start Point	Steway Lane, St Catherine's Valley, Batheaston. Approx. 100m east of junction with Steway Lane and Northend, beside the public footpath entrance. GR: ST780682
Local Café	The Raft Café Boat, Tyning Road, Bathampton, Bath BA2 6TQ ☎ 07733 336989

St Catherine's Valley, a tiny and isolated cleft between hillsides, is home to a couple of excellent climbs, with Steway Lane being the first you'll reach if you're coming from Bath. St Catherine Court, just along the valley, was the home of actress Jane Seymour who built a recording studio here. Since the 1990s, bands including The Cure and Radiohead have beaten a path to the door of this beautiful sixteenth-century manor, with Radiohead producing 'OK Computer' here in 1997.

Like its badly-behaved sister Ayford Lane (Climb 2), Steway Lane is one of those climbs memorable as much for its surface in bad weather as it is for its length or gradient. On the steep parts, this sunken and narrow lane won't have you so much climbing the valley side as desperately scrabbling your way up it, struggling to stay upright and moving as your rear wheel struggles for grip. As you fight your way up the last few hundred metres to the top, it may be helpful to hum the tune of Radiohead's 'No Surprises' to take your mind off the pain in your legs.

THE CLIMB

At around 20 per cent, the first 200m will certainly have you working, but this harsh introduction is short-lived as it quickly drops to around 10 per cent past the cottages. You'll likely still be hurting here, but stay with it because the gradient shortly reverses

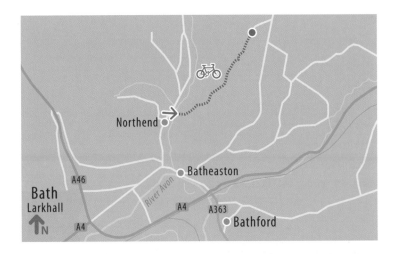

to a gentle downhill that sweeps you along for the next 250m. Enjoy this because, as the open countryside gives way to a high bank and trees begin to enclose the lane, the gradient turns fiercely up. From here it's hard going, with the slope touching 25 per cent in places. It's far from easy in the dry, but if the lane is wet, the mud and stones will only add to your problems as you pick your way up. You've got about 800m of this before you'll feel the gradient reducing as you finally clear the trees and pass the farm. Press on for another 150m to the finish on the bend ahead, beside the left-hand field gate.

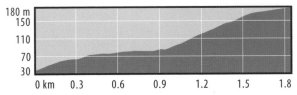

43. THE WRANGLE

Difficulty	◎◎◎◎◎◎◎○○○
Distance	13km
Av. Gradient	11%
Max. Gradient	20%
Height Gain	138m
Road Surface	Moderate/Poor
Start Point	Bottom of Highfield lane, junction with The Street (A368). Approx. 1.5km west of West Harptree. GR: ST546570
Local Café	The Stables Tea room, New Manor Farm, West Harptree, Somerset BS40 6HW ☎ 01761 220172

Just along the road from Harptree Hill (Climb 21) lurks The Wrangle. The name of the road is actually Highfield Lane, but it enjoys this more intriguing local nickname after the small hamlet that sits around the attractive grassy area near the top. While The Wrangle scales the same ridge as Harptree and shares its character, it has some differences, with much of the steepest part wriggling its way to the top through a narrow, sunken lane overhung by a gnarly and dense patch of tree cover. Further interest is provided by the condition of the road under the trees. This, particularly in wet weather, is likely to offer an additional challenge.

THE CLIMB

There's no run-up here. From the junction you'll be working against a gradient that begins at around 10 per cent and quickly rises to 15 per cent within the first 200m. Then, as you round the first bend and just before you enter a tunnel of trees, the slope kicks up briefly to nearly 20 per cent before settling back to around 15 per cent which, while not excessive, is steep enough, because in the woods the road narrows and the quality of the surface declines noticeably. Except for a very brief intermission, there is little relief here from the gradient as the lane writhes and kicks its way upward. For the 500m that you're in the woods, poor weather will mean you're likely to find your rear

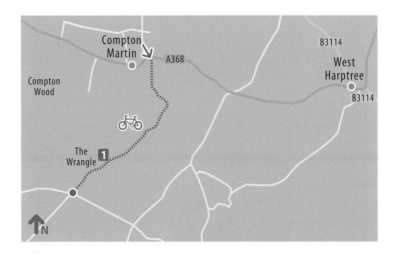

wheel scrabbling for grip as you pick your way around the gravel, wet leaves and mud. Despite the gradient remaining unchanged, it will be with a feeling of relief that you're finally released into an oddly suburban area of clipped hedges and verges that open out onto a common. As you pass the houses, the road surface improves dramatically and although you'll still be pushing against a slope of over 10 per cent in places, you'll

sense you're nearing the top. You'll leave most of the houses behind with about 300m to go and from there to the finish, the gradient eases off to end at the T-junction.

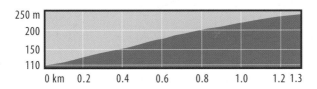

44. TWO TREES

Difficulty	◉◉◉◉◉◉○○○○
Distance	1.8km
Av. Gradient	8%
Max. Gradient	15%
Height Gain	96m
Road Surface	Moderate/Good
Start Point	Blagdon village; junction of High Street (A368) and Street End. GR: ST500589
Local Café	The Burrington Inn, Burrington Combe, North Somerset BS40 7AT ☎ 0761 462227

Two Trees is also known as Blagdon Hill, after the village it climbs upwards from. It's actually made up from three different lanes, the last of which is Two Trees, the

romantically named, ruler-straight stretch of hill that takes you the final kilometre to the top. This hill is the last of the line of climbs of a particular character that scale the northern perimeter of the Mendip Hills. The next one to the west is Burrington Combe (Climb 8) which, with its dramatically soaring limestone cliffs and gently stepped gradient, has a very different character indeed.

THE CLIMB

Because you're already perched a third of the way up the northern flank of the Mendip Hills

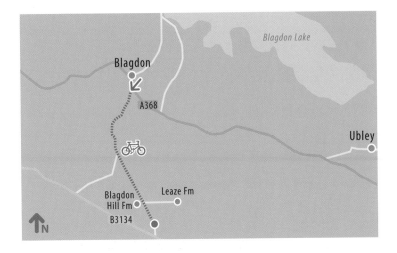

when you set off, you'll be climbing this one from the very first pedal stroke. Straight away you'll be pushing up a 15 per cent gradient that, as you leave the village centre, reduces slightly to around 10 per cent and, as the houses thin out, briefly softens again. From here, the gradient kicks up as you near a series of gentle bends. Then, as the road continues to snake towards the top, this reduces again slightly to around 8 or 9 per cent. This grade remains fairly consistent now for most of the next kilometre and if you look up for a moment you'll see the tree-bordered tarmac stretching away into the distance. This is Two Trees and if the earlier approach had been a lot tougher this would be a dispiriting moment. With any luck though and assuming you haven't gone berserk up the previous 800m, a bit of concentration and commitment should get you through the next several minutes in reasonable condition. As you approach the top there is a final dig that you'll be able to see from some distance. Don't worry too much about this because it's only brief and if you push on just past it over the brow, about 100m before the junction, between two opposing field gates, lies the finish.

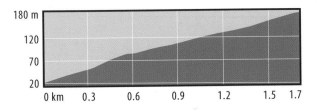

FROM TAUNTON TO BATH BY BICYCLE

If you took a light aircraft from Bristol Airport, it would probably take less than two hours to make a tour of the area covered by this book. The views would be terrific, but it would be two hours that would not do real justice to the enormous range of landscapes that were spread out beneath you. It's only on a bicycle that you really get to experience the true texture and intricate form of the landscape as you move through it.

From Exmoor, dark high and forbidding in its southwestern corner, to the inviting hedge-rowed lanes of its north-eastern-most edge. From the sunny rolling slopes of White Sheet Down and Salisbury Plain in the southeast, to the urban street climbs of Bristol, with, rising between them all, the work-scarred and time-softened Mendip Hills. The topographic richness and diversity of the landscape of this small area is difficult to appreciate without a bicycle.

But this region is not just about a landscape identified by its different hills; it's also about other contrasts. Let's imagine a cyclist setting off northeast from Taunton on a summer's morning, taking a steady ride to Bath. Straight away they will find themselves not struggling against a gradient, but spinning along the oddly criss-crossing roads of the pan-flat peat lands of the Somerset Levels. A place once drained and ditched for cultivation and habitation in past centuries by people whose knowledge of their place in the landscape, while profound, went only as far as their feet could take them in a day.

By lunchtime, our cyclist will have encountered and then ridden up the verdant and soaring 300 metre western flank of the Mendip Hills before traversing the ancient, craggy limestone moorland at its top, still pock-marked by early man and ancient Roman industry. By early afternoon and pressing on toward Bath, they will find the landscape changing again. As The Mendips recede, taking with them their wide views and long steady hills, the land makes way for narrow wooded coombs, tucked away fields and short, twisty climbs.

Finally, nearing Bath from the southwest, this new and distinctive wrinkled and forested landscape, almost claustrophobic in its deepest valleys, intensi-

fies even further. The picturesque scenery and the chocolate-box cottages give little clue to this place's industrial past. Victorian rail bridges, coal-mines and canals, their derelict and empty locks, once marvelled at by travellers and writers when they stood for utility and purpose, now enfolded and reclaimed forever by the woods, trees and meadows that give a different kind of interest to more modern visitors.

By the middle of the afternoon, our cyclist will now be discovering, if they didn't know it already, that the grand City of Bath, clustered around the ancient hot springs that give it its name, settles in an enclosing basin of steep hills and for anyone wishing to get over their rim, one final hard effort is required.

Then at last, as they crest that last climb and they drop down the long descent into the bustling, honey-coloured streets of a city that two centuries ago set the architectural standards for the next hundred years, our cyclist might reflect that in just a handful of hours of riding they have passed through not just several thousand years of continual human history and habitation, but also across some of the most diverse landscape in all of England.

45. VALE STREET

Difficulty	◉◉◉◉◉○○○○○
Distance	100m
Av. Gradient	25%
Max. Gradient	28%
Road Surface	Good
Start Point	Junction of Park Street and Vale Street, Totterdown, Bristol. GR: ST603714
Local Café	Gallery Café, 141 Wells Road, Bristol BS4 2BU ☎ 01179 776639

It's a wry local joke that whoever coined the expression, 'the Seven Hills of Bristol', had obviously never ridden a bike around the place. From both sides of the River Avon the city is riddled with little climbs, many very steep. Count-less Victorian terraces scale the hills as their ranks of painted front doors step one upon the other to the top, scrambling franti-cally upward from the banks of the Avon River. Totterdown in South Bristol contains several of these roads and it is here, tucked in

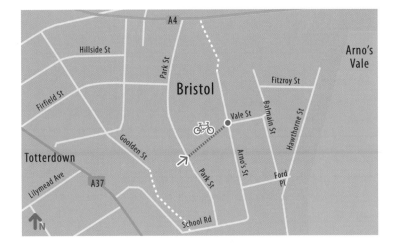

an unremarkable corner of this aptly named Victorian suburb that lurks what purports to be the steepest residential street in Britain.

Others make claims for this title too, but Vale Street certainly is steep and its notoriety alone guarantees it inclusion in this book. At just 100m, a low enough gear and the briefest of run-ups should ensure you'll make it to the top before your legs realize what's going on and start to make too much fuss. If it were much longer I think most people would be in serious difficulties past about 200m. If you do want an extra challenge then try starting from the bottom of the adjacent and also very steep Park Street. This will give you a tough 300-metre climb before you turn into Vale Street and begin the main event.

THE CLIMB

If you are having any doubts about getting to the top of this one, then I'd recommend rolling into Vale Street from just above the junction and staying to the right side of the corner. Then, once you're on the climb proper, just grit your teeth and get those pedals turning. Total commitment is what this one's about and any easing up of the power will be punished by a fairly instantaneous grinding to a stop. The gradient is well in excess of 25 per cent and probably around or above 30 per cent by the steps. This doesn't really back off until you make the end at the junction above you, so just keep it going to the finish.

46. WESTFIELD LANE

Difficulty	◉◉◉◉◉◉◉○○○
Distance	2.2km
Av. Gradient	8%
Max. Gradient	18%
Height Gain	194m
Road Surface	Good
Start Point	Rodney Stoke, approx. 8km north-west of Wells. Junction of Westfield Lane and A371, 100m north-west of entrance to caravan site. GR: ST489497
Local Café	The Café, Myrtle House, Bath Street, Cheddar, Somerset BS27 3AA ☎ 01934 741171

There are a couple of ways up this side of the Mendip Hills if you're on a bicycle and although this route is longer, it is a lot less demanding than its evil sister New Road (Climb 30), just a few kilometres north. That said, if you're looking for a more drawn out and nuanced challenge rather than the interminably brutal leg-wrecker that is New Road, then Westfield Lane might be your choice. It can still boast a kick or two, but there are also moments when the gradient shows a little compassion and your legs get a chance to regain some strength.

On your way to the top on the right you'll pass the disused Westbury Quarry. First recorded as quarrying limestone in the late-nineteenth century, it was last worked in 2003 and is now a Site of Special Scientific Interest.

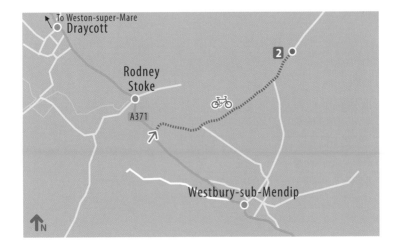

THE CLIMB

With its steady grind of a little under 10 per cent, the first 150m up to the bend sets the tone for much of the next 2km. The slope eases off as you pass the house, but soon returns as you leave the environs of the caravan site and start making your way first parallel to the hilltop and then, with a slow swing left, up the hill itself. This second long bend marks another chance for a breather as the gradient relaxes again before the climb finally begins to take itself seriously. From here, the road steadily tilts up and then settles to a hard, gently snaking climb to the top. While the gradient mostly inclines at between 9 and 15 per cent, you'll still need to keep something in reserve because in places towards the top you'll find it touching 18 per cent, before finally easing off a little as you approach a clearly defined ridge above you that marks the top. The climb ends beside a field gate on your left.

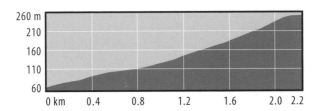

47. WIDCOMBE HILL

Difficulty	⊙⊙⊙⊙⊙⊙○○○○
Distance	1.7km
Av. Gradient	9%
Max. Gradient	15%
Height Gain	151m
Road Surface	Good
Start Point	Bottom of Widcombe Hill, Bath. Junction with Pulteney Road, A36. GR: ST755642
Local Café	Secret Garden Café, Prior Park Road, Bath BA2 4NF ☎ 01225 789788

One of the best and possibly unique features of the city of Bath is that the countryside extends almost to the city centre. This is particularly true in the beautiful Widcombe area where sheep graze the precipitous hills less than a kilometre from the bustling city centre. Within 800m, this climb lifts you quickly away from the busy Pulteney Road, past ranks of high-walled Georgian villas and out into National Trust country-side. With its verdant hills tumbling down past you back towards the city it's worth a glance over your shoulder as you grind your way past the meadows because the view from here, little changed for over two centuries, is a good one.

THE CLIMB

Widcombe Hill begins on a 10 per cent slope that barely lets up to the top. In fact, as you climb slowly past the buildings on its lower slopes and by the time you've covered 400m, you'll find the gradient has increased to around 14 per cent. But the slope set-tles back quickly, and as the houses start to thin out, the gradient reduces to a more or less constant 10 per cent. For most of its length the road is fairly wide and with few bends. This means you'll get plenty of opportunity to contemplate the unremitting slope ahead of you.

 With the houses behind you and with just over a kilometre to go, the trees open out to meadows and woodland and as you push on towards more trees and past a row of Regency villas, you can comfort yourself knowing you are over halfway up.

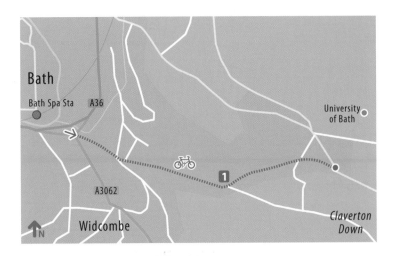

The closing moves of this climb take place through 400m of dense woodland bordered by low stone walls. Here the gradient continues to work away at your legs, only beginning to slacken noticeably as you emerge from the woods. The end is at the second left-hand junction 200 metres or so beyond the trees.

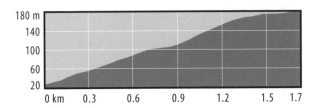

48. WINFORD LANE

Difficulty	●●●●●○○○○○
Distance	1km
Av. Gradient	9%
Max. Gradient	20%
Height Gain	83m
Road Surface	Poor/Moderate
Start Point	Bottom of Winford Lane at field gates, Winford Approx. 1km south-west of Bishopsworth. GR: ST477656
Local Café	Moondance, 5 South Parade, Chew Magna, Bristol BS40 8SH ☎ 01275 331173

The 233-metre Dundry Hill looms over south-west Bristol, its slopes offering cyclists several opportunities to test themselves on climbs of varying severity. One of the

least demanding of these is probably Winford Lane, which scales Dundry's less precipitous southern flank. The road takes you nearly to the edge of the village of Dundry and once you're up, be sure to reward yourself with the hill's fabled and magnificent views of the city of Bristol and the Welsh mountains beyond.

Winford Lane is strange. It actually begins life as Dundry Lane as it winds out of Winford village. It is only a kilometre later that two adjacent signs inform you that 'Dundry' has become 'Winford'. So take it easy and try to ignore the bit of climbing and descending you need to do when you leave the village because it is only after this, at the signs, that the climb begins.

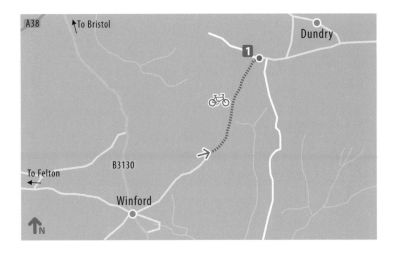

THE CLIMB

After 150m, the initial gentle approach soon develops into something more testing as the road starts to turn up to a gradient of around 16 per cent. This continues for the next 200m until the lane levels momentarily before rearing up again. This 16 per cent rise slowly transforms itself into an increasingly testing section that peaks at around 20 per cent before quickly dropping again to 7 per cent. The lane follows a similar pattern past a converted barn on the right, with regular changes in gradient requiring repeated adjustments in tempo. After the barn, the gradient drops away to around 3 per cent before kicking up again to about 8 per cent for the last time as you approach a bungalow on the bend. Continue past here for another 60m along a gentle gradient to finish at the junction.

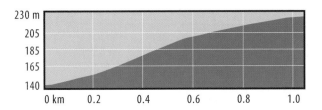

49. WINSLEY HILL

Difficulty	⦿⦿⦿⦿⦿⦿○○○○
Distance	1.2km
Av. Gradient	10%
Max. Gradient	14%
Height Gain	91m
Road Surface	Good
Start Point	Winsley Hill (B3108), Limpley Stoke. Just after bridge over river, approx. 100m east of rail bridge. GR: ST782612
Local Café	The Angelfish, Brassknocker Hill, Monkton Combe, Bath BA2 7JD ☎ 01225 723483

If you want to head anywhere out of Bath on a bike and you don't want to have to fight with the trucks, cars and buses on the A4, then pretty soon you'll be going up hill. Steeply and often. The riders in the 2014 edition of the Tour of Britain discovered this on Stage 6 when they left Bath for Hemel Hempstead. After a quick tour past the sights, the peloton was directed south up the Wellsway, a long, two-part climb out of the city. They then moved on to what is likely to have been a record-breaking descent of the vertiginous Brassknocker Hill (Climb 4). This brought them to the edge of the River Avon and to the bottom of Winsley Hill, a broad, gently winding climb up the opposite hillside. It was a long stage that day, 215km, but to judge by the speed the leading riders launched themselves up this not-unimpressive hill, the miles they still had ahead weren't worrying any of them unduly.

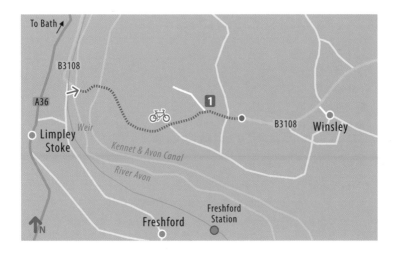

THE CLIMB

From the start, as the road bends left ahead, you'll find yourself on a 10 per cent gradient. Then, as you cross the canal and the road swings right, this increases to around 13 per cent. You'll have about 300m of this until, as a row of houses appear on the right, like a gentle torture the gradient increases slightly again. You're likely to be feeling uncomfortable here because there has been no let up since the bottom, a good 500 metres earlier. As you pass the houses, you'll feel the slope reduce noticeably to around 7 per cent. Here the trees give way to a high stone wall and open fields. But don't get complacent as you feel the pressure on your legs easing. As the top of the hill approaches it kicks again up to 10 per cent, giving your legs a final workout before the hill eases back over the last couple of hundred metres to the top beside an overgrown track to your right.

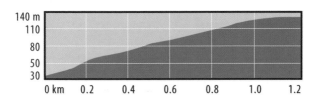

50. WOODS HILL

Difficulty	⬤⬤⬤⬤⬤◯◯◯◯◯
Distance	0.4km
Av. Gradient	14%
Max. Gradient	25%
Height Gain	56m
Road Surface	Moderate
Start Point	The Hop Pole Inn, Limpley Stoke. Approx. 2.5km south-east of Bath. GR: ST781610
Local Café	The Angelfish, Brassknocker Hill, Monkton Combe, Bath BA2 7JD ☎ 01225 723483

This is a great climb for anyone who wants to savour the delights of a steep ascent but would prefer to find out what 'steep' actually means on a bike before they set off up some of the much longer and far tougher challenges in this book. The two testing sections are both short with a reasonable respite between them and at 400m, the finish should arrive well before your legs completely disintegrate.

As you prepare to do battle, take the chance to look around you. In 1989, Kazuo Ishiguro's acclaimed film *The Remains of the Day* used the Hop Pole Inn and the adjacent street as a location for some of the scenes. There must be something about this area because in 1953, Charles Crichton filmed much of his comedy *The Titfield Thunderbolt* here too.

Be aware, the finish at the very top of the final steep stretch will pop you straight out onto the often busy and truck-infested A36. I'd strongly suggest pulling into one of the drives close to the top rather than triumphantly propelling yourself across the junction here.

THE CLIMB

Just getting started on this one is a challenge. It's more or less 25 per cent from the off, but hang in there because once you get going, the sharp turn just 70m ahead marks the end of this first hard test. As you round the corner here, the gradient more than halves and there follows a gently snaking 200-metre climb of a little under 10 per cent

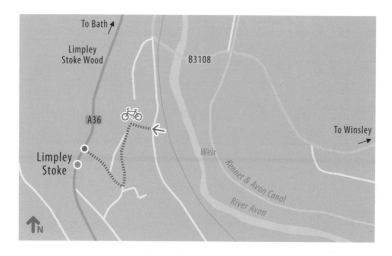

to the hairpin ahead. Don't get carried away as you approach this bend though, because the final steep stretch lurks just around the corner. It's around 130m long and at getting on for 20 per cent all the way to the top, you'll need something left for the last hard push to the finish at the junction above you.

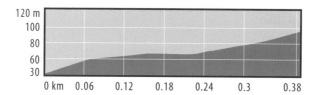

LOCAL BIKE SHOPS

BRISTOL

Bike UK
First Floor, Embassy House, Queen's Avenue,
Bristol BS8 1SB
0117 9293500

Evans Cycles
Lewins Mead, Bristol BS1 2PY
0117 9277639

Jake's Bikes
6A Haymarket Walk, Bristol BS1 3LN
0117 3297363

Mud Dock Cycleworks
40 The Grove, Bristol BS1 4RB
0117 9292151

Pembury Cycles
8 Highridge Road, Bishopsworth, Bristol
BS13 8HA
0117 9640973

Strada Cycles
236 North Street, Southville, Bristol BS3 1JD
0117 9669662

NORTH EAST

Avon Valley Cyclery
Brunel Square, Bath BA1 1SX
01225 442442

Cadence Bike Shop
9 Chelsea Road. Bath BA1 3PP
01225 446887

Cycology
20 New Road, Chippenham, Wiltshire
SN15 1HS
01249 461997

Hares Cycleworks
6 High Street, Weston Village, Bath BA1 4BX
01225 422674

John's Bikes
84 Walcot Street, Bath BA1 5BD
01225 581666

Total Fitness
3 Saracen Street, Bath BA1 5BR
01225 444164

SOUTH EAST

Batchelors
24 Market Place, Warminster, Wiltshire
BA12 9AN
01985 213221

Hammoon Cycles
24J Wincombe Business Park, Shaftesbury
SP7 9QJ
01747 850622

Live2Ride
The Old Courthouse, Waterloo, Frome,
Somerset BA11 3FE
01373 469590

SOUTH WEST

Pompy's Cycles
Mart Road, Minehead TA24 5BJ
01643 704077

Porlock Pedals
The Old Tannery, High Street, Porlock
TA24 8PU
01643 863212

The Bicycle Chain
Salmon Parade, Bridgwater TA6 5PY
01278 423640

CENTRAL

Bad Ass Bikes
Burrington Combe, Bristol BS40 7AT
01761 462011

Bike City
8 Queen Street, Wells BA5 2DP
01749 670002

Cheddar Cycle Store
1E Valley Line Industrial Park, Wedmore Road,
Cheddar, Somerset BS27 3EE
01934 741300